D1499387

HUNTING ON HORSEBACK

DEDICATION

To my wife, Kat, who had faith when all around faltered.

TO THE READER

Anyone having questions or requiring additional information is invited to write to me at Paladin Press.

Jim Ottman

HUNTING ON HORSEBACK

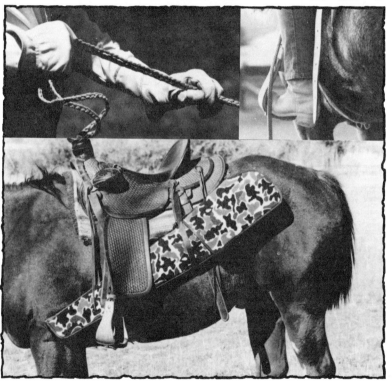

JIM OTTMAN

PALADIN PRESS
BOULDER, COLORADO

Hunting on Horseback
by Jim Ottman
Copyright © 1987 by Jim Ottman

ISBN 0-87364-427-1
Printed in the United States of America

Published by Paladin Press, a division of
Paladin Enterprises, Inc., P.O. Box 1307
Boulder, Colorado 80306, USA.
(303) 443-7250

Direct inquiries and/or orders to the above address.

Illustrations by Anne Mace.
Photos on pages 60–70 by Barb Beasley.
Models: Ronni Britton (p. 6)
         Kathy Ottman (pp. 11, 15, 119, 124)
         Tom Laidlaw (pp. 60–70)

Contents

Foreword

If you are seriously interested in hunting on horseback, this book is for you. It offers a wealth of information for both the newcomer and the experienced hunter. Read the whole book. As you progress from one chapter to the next, you will gain confidence as each becomes a stepping-stone to increase your hunting knowledge and enjoyment.

Author Jim Ottman will help you set your goals and reach them, saving you time and money in the preparation of your hunt. Jim takes you out there with his personal experience in such a way that you won't make the mistakes so common to the beginner.

You'll learn about finding and booking a reliable guide and outfitter, how to communicate with them, and what responsibilities you must share with each other.

Clothing and equipment—so critical to the horseback hunter—are carefully considered in such a way as to help you minimize excess baggage without endangering your health, comfort, and safety on the trip.

As the planning of the hunt progresses, you will gain confidence as you prepare and practice correctly, covering such additional needs as licenses, permits, transportation, and how to find reliable help in the area you wish to hunt.

Then the book—along with easy-to-follow photos—carefully takes you into a program of physical conditioning geared specifically for your hunt on horseback. These often overlooked exercises can make your hunt on horseback a pleasure instead of the miserable experience so often endured by the poorly conditioned hunter. Ottman removes the mysteries of camping on horseback in an honest, straightforward manner, discussing differences in camping situations for your personal preferences. Convenient checklists of camping needs are provided as well.

The art of packing with horses is covered in detail, showing the hunter how much he can pack out sensibly and how to properly prepare the animals and equipment. You'll also learn how to become familiar with the horses you will be riding and working with. Anyone, from novice to expert, who plans to hunt on horseback will find the chapter on tack and equipment especially helpful. The author leaves little to the imagination as he covers this often confusing topic.

Ottman also provides his views on rifles and ammunition for the hunter on horseback in a sensible and logical manner that allows you to make your own final decisions. He covers the special areas to consider when selecting a rifle and ammo for hunting on horseback.

A complete state-by-state and province-by-province (for Canada) listing of game and fish department addresses, along with a guide and outfitter association listing, conclude the book.

If hunting on horseback is one of your endeavors, this book can provide you the information and help you need.

Norman E. Johnson
Columnist, *Sports & Recreation*

Chapter 1
Saddle Up!

For untold centuries, man has stalked his prey with a noble partner—the horse. Medieval knights roamed Europe with steed and lance, slaying wild boars and bear. Roman legionnaires tracked lions with their mighty chargers trained for war. And, as every American schoolboy knows, the wild chase for buffalo across our great frontier was the survival mainstay of the Indians and early pioneers.

Many sportsmen—especially those with a healthy spirit for adventure—continue to relive this ancient hunting art today. Unfortunately, the lessons our ancestors learned don't come easily to anyone, and gaining experience as a mounted hunter can be an arduous task. This book is offered as a shortcut to horseback hunting's school of hard knocks. A million mistakes can be made, and any one of them can turn the hunt of a lifetime into a nightmare. If I haven't made every mistake in the book already, I know someone else who has. With this primer, you can expect to avoid some of the more painful experiences.

Most of today's hunters are not horsemen in everyday life. In days past, riding a horse was as common as driving a car is today. Of course, the mechanics of riding were ingrained in our forefathers as much as braking, accelerating, and steering movements are ingrained in us. Don't think you can take off to hunt on horseback without first learning to ride, or at least breaking yourself in before you go, if you're already a horseman. If you are a non-rider or haven't ridden for many months, your first step should be to throw your leg over a horse and acquaint yourself with the feel of saddle leather pressed against your posterior.

If you are a complete novice, the best solution is to find a stable or riding academy that offers lessons. Also, a knowledgeable friend who owns a horse and will spend the time to instruct you rates high on the list. Failing those options, rent a horse and start the hard way.

Once you have received instruction or gained some experience, the next step is to ride several times a week. Try to extend your rides each time until you can comfortably spend several hours in the saddle without fatigue. It is vitally important that you ride in the type of clothing and footwear that you intend to use on the hunt. You will find that certain items do not sit well in a saddle. Once of the first things to go will be any wallet or other bulky item normally carried in the back pocket. In addition to being uncomfortable, such items have a terrible habit of sliding out of your pocket and onto the ground at the furthest point in your ride. By the same token, you never miss them until you are back at the corral. By all means, do not ride in tennis shoes, running shoes, etc. Wearing any heel-less footwear in a stirrup is asking for trouble. Proper clothing for riding is covered more specifically in Chapter Three.

One of the major things to come to your attention as you begin riding for the first time is that the backside is not the part of the anatomy which needs toughening. By the end of a short ride the legs, inside of the knees, and the lower back muscles will feel like they are on fire. After determining your own points of muscular deficiency, you will be able to form the basis for a regular exercise program. See Chapter Five for specific guides.

As you progress on your riding skills at the stable or friend's ranch, one of the first things you should insist on is

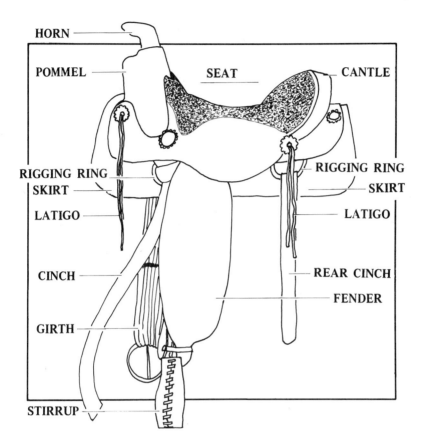

HORN

POMMEL — SEAT — CANTLE

RIGGING RING — RIGGING RING
SKIRT — SKIRT
LATIGO — LATIGO

CINCH — REAR CINCH
— FENDER

GIRTH

STIRRUP

A typical saddle, labeled to show each part.

saddling your own horse. There are few things worse than finding yourself alone, five miles from camp, with a loose cinch strap and no idea how to tighten it. You will find yourself taking a long walk home, or, worse, getting hurt in the process of trying to ride a loose saddle.

The same situation exists with bridles. Some horses develop a knack for rubbing their headstalls off on any solid object they can find. If you can't replace it, you can't ride. You may even lose the horse in the bargain. Saddling and bridling are not complicated procedures once you master them, but they are not tasks at which you can become an expert on the first try.

With the horse firmly tied to a strong support, pick up the saddle blanket or pad and, working from the horse's left side, place the blanket squarely on the animal's back. Make sure the blanket is centered and free of wrinkles. Then, pick up the saddle by the horn and the cantle and toss it onto the animal with an upward and downward motion so that it comes to rest firmly in the correct position. In order to avoid spooking a shy horse, it is a good idea to pull the right stirrup and the cinch up over the top of the saddle and hold them until the saddle is resting on the horse. Then, ease them down slowly into position so as to avoid slapping the horse with the two heavy pieces of tack.

Check once more for centering of both blanket and saddle. Once they are in place, reach under the horse's chest just behind the front legs and pull the cinch band to the left side. Make sure that it is not twisted or hung up before you proceed further. When everything is in shape, put the left-side cinch strap through the O-ring of the belly band and take up the slack. Depending on the length of the strap in relation to the horse's girth, it may require one or two loops through the rings before securing the cinch to prevent having a loose cinch strap to contend with. Follow the diagram to secure the cinch in place. There are other methods of cinching, but the one illustrated is simple and secure enough for any horse-back-hunting situation.

As you tighten the cinch strap, bear in mind that a horse may suck enough air during the process to leave several inches of slack in the cinch after the nag exhales. Always recheck the cinch after the horse has stood for a few minutes to see if you can pull any more slack out of the strap. Also, watch the animal for any puffing of the belly as you cinch; when you're ready to really screw the leather down, give the critter a sharp knee in the paunch and pull at the same instant. It is a good idea to stop and check your cinch for slack after a few minutes of riding until you get to the point at which you can feel the saddle placement from the seat.

Some saddles have a second cinch strap on the rear. These

The proper way to cinch a saddle.

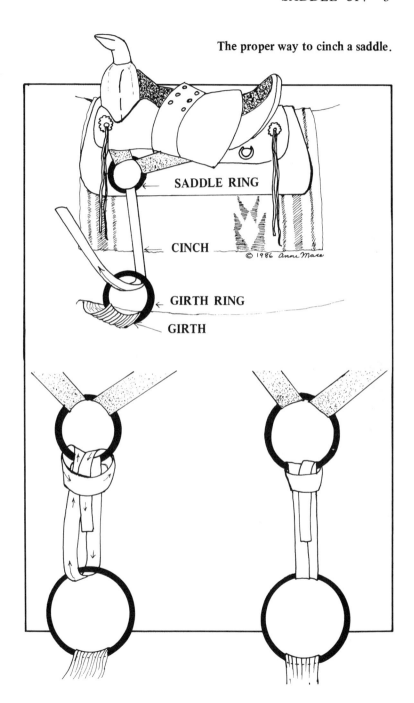

SADDLE RING

CINCH

© 1986 anne mace

GIRTH RING

GIRTH

belly cinches are primarily to prevent a saddle from being jerked forward when a steer hits the end of a lariat at a gallop. If your saddle is of this double-rigged style, don't leave too much slack in the rear cinch, but don't make it too tight, either. Sucking every inch of slack that you can possibly get out of the rear cinch is next to a guarantee that you will turn the pleasure ride into a bucking contest.

Setting a stirrup can be a frustrating experience for the new rider. It often entails getting off and on the animal numerous times, trying to guess where to start. A simple way to get into the ballpark is to place the stirrup itself under your armpit, reach up the leather along the fender, and see if your fingertips come close to the outer edge of the saddle's seat. If so, you can be pretty sure that you will have only one or two adjustments to make from that point on, depending on the girth of the horse. The stirrups should be set at a length that allows you to stand up in the saddle with about a hand's breadth between your pelvis and the seat.

The length of your arm will get you within one adjustment of the proper stirrup position when you ride.

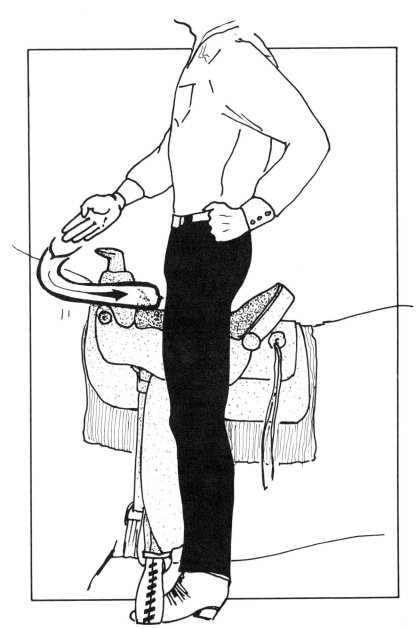

Proper seating requires about three to four inches of space between pelvis and saddle as you stand in the stirrups.

A stirrup which is too long will offer you no control from the seat in terms of balance or as a cushion against shock. A stirrup which is too short will do the same thing, plus give you sore knees in no time.

The bridle may be of so many designs, and carry such an assortment of bits, that it would be impossible to cover every option here. If the bit has a mouth bar that must be placed in the horse's mouth, the easiest way to do so is to stick your thumb into the rearmost corner of the animal's mouth and apply a little pressure until he opens his mouth. There are no teeth way back near the cheek so don't worry about being bitten. When the animal does open his mouth, slip the bit in and push the headstall up over the ears. Adjust the brow band and then check to make sure that nothing is twisted. If all is correct, reach under the neck to find the dangling throat strap and secure it to the buckle on the left side of the bridle. Do not over-tighten this band, simply snug it into place and remember into which hole the buckle needs to fit each time thereafter. If you are using a metal bit and the weather is cold, be sure to warm the bit in your hands prior to inserting it into the horse's mouth. Failing to do so causes pain for the horse equal to you putting your tongue on a metal pump handle in subzero temperatures.

Once you have become proficient at saddling and bridling, practice doing so in the dark. Many hunting-camp activities take place in the black of night. Ready in the pre-dawn and home after dusk has fallen is the only way to take advantage of the two best hunting times of the day—sunup and sundown. In order to be where the game is at the right time, you have to get ready and travel in the dark. Don't depend on someone else to take care of these tasks for you. To avoid wasted time and possible injury, learn them yourself.

There are many ways to manipulate a horse—posture, leg control, and various reining techniques. For the purposes to which you are striving, the easiest advice to follow is not to keep the reins too tight. Most trained horses are capable of working with little or no guidance. A tense set of reins will cause you more harm than good, for the horse will be con-

Taking up the slack in the reins is easily accomplished with your free hand in an emergency.

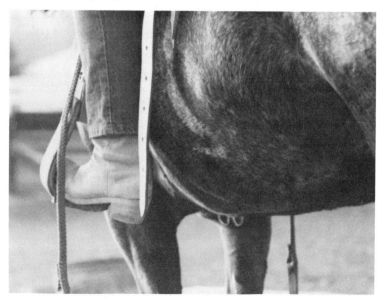

You can use heel pressure to cue your horse as well as reining. Note the proper position of the foot in the stirrup.

stantly confused and fighting the bit. The more hazardous
the going gets, the more the horse needs its head. You will
find that the animal is more adept at finding the best footing
than you are. The reins should have a slight droop between
your hands and the bit as you sit in the saddle. If you run
the reins through the fingers of your left hand, you can use
your right hand to pull up the slack should the need develop
to really put the pressure on.

Most string animals used by an outfitter will be very plod-
ding and docile, content to follow almost anywhere without
urging. On the other hand, trying to rein one of them away
from the guide's mount may be more than the inexperienced
rider can handle.

While most neophytes tend to use drive reining, most
saddle horses are trained to neck rein. The basic difference is
that in drive reining, you pull the rein on the side you wish to
turn toward, i.e., left rein left, right rein right. Neck reining
is simply a cue produced by laying the rein against the
horse's neck on the opposite side of the turning direction,
and letting the horse move away from it, i.e., right rein on
horse's neck to turn left. Minimal pressure is required to
cue a well-trained horse.

While on the topic of reins, there are pros and cons to both
sides of the "tied-end" controversy. By tying the rein ends
together, you can let go of them without losing one or both.
This is quite important when it comes to using your binoculars, or getting your maps or compass out. On the other hand,
if you let the reins fall, you have a better chance of retrieving
a wandering horse. By watching each time the horse steps
onto a loose rein end and then yelling *whoa!* just as he snubs
up on the rein, you can usually gather him up without a
mile-long chase. The decision of which method to use is
yours to make.

By all means, never trust the reins as a means of securing
your horse to an object for any period of time. This method
only works well in the movies and with a carefully trained
horse. Leave the halter on under the bridle and carry a good,
solid lead rope. Use it to anchor that bangtail to something

Tying your reins makes their loss from the saddle less likely.

Loose reins allow an easier catch of a wandering horse.

substantial. Not only can a horse move immense loads, but flimsy supports like car doors are only so much balsa wood when the animal really desires to depart the area. Given the willpower and leverage to do so, a horse can snap almost anything.

I once broke a mustang named Mac. In one afternoon under the hot Wyoming sun, that ornery cuss snapped a 3/8-inch lariat three times in a row while snubbed to a twelve-by-twelve-inch post. Ol' Mac was an Appy (Appaloosa) mustang straight off the open range, and he turned out to be one of the best elk-hunting horses I ever owned. His only problem was a fear of the color white. If anything white ever crossed his path at closer than ten feet, we made a mystical end change in midair. Still another old pony, named Pal because of his pure Palamino lineage, hated water. Katy Jane didn't like mud, and Penney spooked over anything loose on the saddle. I tell you these things only to point out to novice and experienced rider alike that every horse has its idiosyncrasies. Know them ahead of time, or you're liable to get hurt!

When tying off a horse, if you get a guilty feeling in your gut about tying him off on only a three-foot lead, and therefore get the urge to let him roam around on a ten- or twenty-foot rope so he can graze while you're gone, stop and watch closely as a nag twines its way back and forth on a long lead rope. You'll soon see how many times that rope gets wrapped around its legs, and if the horse panics, you'll also see a perfectly good animal lamed, or worse. It's much better to tie off short and high, and have a ridable horse when you return. Because of this, forsake your own ideas of humanity and tie off with a lead about three feet in length, about five feet above the ground.

To give you still another illustration of the trouble long leads can get you into, I recall a time on an early-season elk hunt when I nearly lost a sorrel mare to a long lead. We had stopped to sneak to the ridgeline and glass the next valley and the mountainsides. Both horses were old hands at such endeavors and we tied them with ten feet of rope to "quakies" (quaking aspen trees) so they could graze. I happened to come back early to the horses and was watching two bear cubs in the valley below when the mare stepped over the rope with both hind feet. When she raised her head, the rope tightened up and she jerked harder. Both hind legs went up under her belly, and she hit the ground like a ton of bricks, with her nose tucked up under her right shoulder, snug against that rope. The harder she pulled, the tighter the rope snubbed her nose and legs up under her. I ended up having to cut the rope in two in order to save her from suffocating herself. If I had not been sitting right there, we would have had a dead horse, twenty miles from nowhere.

Now that we have the novice rider working on his horsemanship skills, let's turn our attention to the hunter who intends to use a personal horse for the hunt. If you've never hunted with the horse before, there are several things to bear in mind. Just like you, that mass of four-legged muscle needs to be toughened up and put into shape prior to the actual hunt. Don't expect a pleasure horse that has been ridden once a week for an hour to be ready to climb mountains with you in the saddle. In fact, he'll be lucky to be able to walk all day long, for several days, on the level without a conditioning period. Ride your animal every day if possible. Make each ride longer and more strenuous than the one before.

When you have the animal in top shape, you may think that you are now ready to go hunting. Wrong! When you reach that level of performance, it is time to start adding unknowns to your rides. If you remember what I said about certain hunting horses and their quirks, you'll start getting into the swing of things.

Ride in trees and heavy brush. Ride in streams and ponds of varying depths. See how the horse reacts to snapping twigs and dry leaves. Watch him during a thunderstorm to see if the thunder and lightning spook him. Determine how driven sand and dust affect the animal. Attempt to simulate any conditions you may face on the hunt. Wooden bridges are very likely; consider the hollow sound they produce when ridden across. By locating problems and potential problems now, you have the time to iron them out while you still have the chance to do so. Solve as many problems as possible before the hunt—don't wait until you're in the middle of the wilderness with your life hanging by a slender thread.

Speaking of thunderstorms, one of the worst places you can be during one is in the saddle. Any time lightning is flashing, dismount and wait it out under some form of protection. Dense overhead vegetation is fine, so long as it isn't part of the highest point in the area. Low areas like creek beds and ditches can protect you and your horse from ground shock. Avoid high trees and rocky points—they draw bolts just like lightning rods.

Lest we forget, now is also the time to get the animal used to gunfire. Take him out and tie him to a very substantial anchor with a lead rope and halter. Start slowly and quietly, preferably with something in the .22 rimfire range. Gradually work up to the caliber you intend to hunt with. Try to make it very obvious to the horse what is about to transpire prior to firing each shot. Horses, like people, tend to shy at the unexpected.

Never shoot from the saddle. Not only are you more apt to end up in a heap on the ground doing so, but you just might shoot your horse. His head can come up much higher than you might expect in a tense situation and can easily enter your line of fire, particularly if you are hunting with a handgun. Horses are for *hunting only*. Once the quarry has been found, do your stalking and shooting on two legs. And another thing, if you don't end up with a dead horse when shooting from the saddle, you will certainly end up with a deaf one. Horses' ears are no different than yours in that respect. Shock waves from a high-powered rifle or pistol will soon deaden the nerves, and you'll have a horse that says, "Huh?" quite frequently. In the same vein, wear ear protection yourself.

Hunting with your horse is different from pleasure riding in many ways. One area often overlooked, until it is too late, is the use of spoken commands. When hunting spooky buck deer or bull elk, one word is all that it takes to send

Shooting from horseback is a no-no.

them over the next ridgeline. Even a whisper is too much of a disturbance under heavy pressure. Spend a lot of time making your horse respond to the reins, and knee and heel cues. Until the day when you can literally ride for hours in total silence and still go exactly where you want to go, when you want to go there, you aren't ready to take that particular hayburner hunting. You should be able to cue every command with your legs and shifts in your body weight. Commands for right and left turns, the degree of the turn, and stop and go, including the speed of the gait, should all become silent and sure between you and the horse. A well-trained hunter and horse can ride right into a herd of elk or up to a bedded deer.

Unless you are more fortunate than most, you will not be able to ride from the corral to the hunting area on horseback. Therefore, it is important for you to make sure during your preparation period that your horse loads and unloads into and out of a trailer or truck without a fight. If he doesn't, you can bet your bottom dollar that you'll spend precious hunting time jerking on a rope and shoving on the south end of a northbound horse on each occasion. Some horses put up a fight at the trailer door from day one. By feeding in the trailer for a time, however, most, but not all, will come to load easily. Having a second horse that does load well, as an example and comfort to the balky one, is sometimes all it takes to solve the dilemma.

By now you have the basic plan for getting ready. There is no way to cover all of the points that will be salient to any given hunt, so plan carefully and start well in advance of your departure date. Even in the corral, good horsemanship takes time. With all the variables and challenges that horseback hunting offers, dedicated and careful training can mean the difference between a great hunt and disaster. Train hard and often with as many realistic hunting conditions as possible. Remember to practice using the identical gear with which you intend to hunt. Not doing so is tantamount to practicing basketball using a fifty-five-gallon barrel for a basket. You might feel real good about the results, but they are next to useless when it comes time to play the actual game.

Chapter 2
Guides & Outfitters

C hoosing your guide or outfitter is an exciting and challenging part of a trophy hunt. Making the right decision requires much more effort and thought than most hunters put into the task. I do not exaggerate when I say that more once-in-a-lifetime hunts are ruined by poor communication than by any other factor.

Begin the process by deciding what it is that you want to hunt, and where. Even if you intend to make it a combination hunt, one of the species is going to have to become the focal point of the quest. Once this is decided, you also need to know if you are going to hunt solo, take a partner, or go with a group. If a partner or a group is involved, or even if you're going alone, you need to get a consensus of opinion on the reason for the trip. Make up your mind that you really want to hunt, not just get away. There are few things more exasperating to a hunting party than to find out, after a hard day's ride into a spike camp, that half of the group wants to spend at least eight hours a day in a bar or off sightseeing.

Having narrowed down your priorities, you must now connect with several outfitters who specialize in the type of hunt you want. Several options are available to you in this search. The best method is to have an outfitter recommended to you by one of your friends who has used the service with good results. Barring this, the listings in Appendix B will give you a starting point. All of the associations listed can supply you with the names of members who work the area you wish to hunt. Another source of information is to write the chamber of commerce in a city near the area where you wish to hunt and ask for a list of reputable outfitters who work in the locale. The Game and Fish Department of the state in which you plan to hunt may also offer listings of licensed guides in a given area. Still more listings can be found in the classified ad sections of national magazines and sporting journals.

If you happen to be a member of a national hunting club, it may have approved listings available which have been used, and approved, by several members. These listings will usually have comments by the member hunters in terms of accommodations, food, game availability, and other pertinent information.

There are also several agencies which will book a hunt for you in the same manner as a travel agent books airline reservations. This is a relatively new way to go hunting. Agencies can be a good bet, as they will intercede for you in the event of major problems with the businesses they represent. Such services are usually free to the hunter.

Your initial contact should be with several different outfitters at once. Even though you are sending out several letters asking the same thing, you are better off to make each one an original rather than a photocopy. Even big business likes to feel special. From the responses, you can begin to narrow the list to fit your requirements.

In your initial letter to a prospective outfitter, you should include the following information and questions to be answered:

1. State the game you wish to hunt, and any limitations you may impose on the trophy. If, for instance, you will only consider a five-point, buck mule deer having no brow tines and perfectly matched sides, say so. If the outfitter cannot provide a likelihood of seeing such an animal, there is no sense going on with the exchange of information.

2. Ask when the best time to plan the hunt would be, and how much time you will need to have for the hunt itself, if indeed there are any bookings left open. Bear in mind that most good outfitters are booked at least a year in advance and many of them for two or more years ahead. You must therefore plan for the future in dealing with them.

3. State what methods you wish to employ on the hunt, and see if they are supplied by that outfitter. As rudimentary as that may sound, it is not out of the realm of possibility to book a hunt you think is on horseback and find on arrival that it is actually by Jeep or ATV. Also, with widely different hunting regulations throughout the country, make sure your weapon and load are legal for the game you are hunting and for the area you wish to hunt in. Problems like these happen because people tend to take things for granted instead of communicating in advance.

4. Ask for price lists in your first contact, what the guide-to-hunter ratio is, and what the extra cost for one guide to one hunter would be, if available at all. Check also on the cost to bring along a non-hunting camp member. Don't expect to bring your non-hunting spouse or child into camp for the week without paying extra.

5. Ask for past success rates for the species you're after in the area you're going to hunt. Ask how long the outfitter has hunted in that specific area. Find out the number of support staff in the camp. No one can guide all day, cook, wash dishes, wrangle horses, and entertain the group around the campfire, and be expected to do any of it well.

6. Most importantly, ask for a list of references and for the number of return bookings the outfitter averages each year. No one continues to book hunts year after year with an unsatisfactory outfit. These references should be hunters who paid their money and took their chances with the same outfitter in prior years. Contact the people in person, or by phone, if at all possible. Folks tend to give you better and more complete information verbally than they will in a letter.

Don't be too surprised if all the names supplied to you

by the firm turn out to be hunters who have taken good trophies. This is only good business on the part of the outfitter; he would be less than bright to supply you with disgruntled clients. However, if you make it a point to request the names of some clients who have not scored, the outfitter should be willing to supply them.

In addition to what these past hunters did or did not tag, ask them about camp conditions, staff attitude, methods used to locate game, and the type, condition, and quality of the equipment supplied. Don't forget the most important question: "Would you go back again?" Ask too, if these hunters can give you the names of others who hunted in the same camp while they were with the outfitter. These secondary contacts will often give you better information than the original references did.

Once you have decided on a specific outfitter, your task becomes one of developing a working knowledge on both sides as to what is expected of each party and who is to supply what. Some specific questions for you to ask at this point are:

1. "Where does my responsibility for transportation to and from the hunting area begin and end?" It can happen that you fly into an airport fifty miles from the base camp, and are then expected to get yourself, your equipment, and any game you may take to and from the airport. While you're at it, find out which airport to fly into. The most logical on the map is not always the correct choice. Decide on an exact spot to be met. There are few things more aggravating than to be waiting at the baggage area while your outfitter is sitting in the concourse bar trying to figure out where you are.

2. "What equipment am I required to supply for myself?" Normally, you should bring your rifle, ammo, bedroll, personal needs, and toilet articles. But what about eating utensils? What about saddlebags, rifle scabbards that fit your rifle, snacks, oversized stirrups, and canteens? The list is endless, but some things you just have to know in advance. *Ask!*

3. "Who is responsible to gut and quarter any game

taken?" If it's you, do you know how, and do you have the needed equipment to do so?

4. "How much gear is allowed on a pack trip per hunter?" Chances are, you can't take in your Franklin stove, but what about suitcases, cases of beer or soft drinks, or an extra rifle? If it's not going in with you, why drag it along in the first place?

5. "Who decides what is an acceptable trophy?" It seems self-evident that it should be the hunter, yet many guides tend to get hostile when they show a client a four-point deer or a herd of elk, and the client refuses to shoot anything because it doesn't meet his goal. Get that perfectly clear before you start.

6. "Is alcohol allowed in camp?" If so, is there a rule about drinking before the day's hunt is over? There ought to be!

7. "Am I going to have any say in hunting technique?" If you book a horseback hunt and find later that the guide doesn't like to ride, who has the final say on which way to hunt? It is a waste of money to hire a guide and then not listen to his advice, but in some matters, it is your money. Why spend money to hunt in a manner directly opposite to that which you wanted?

8. "Is there a cook in camp, or am I expected to share the chore?" The same goes for the care of stock, wood cutting, and packing tasks.

9. "What are the terrain and weather likely to offer, and what should I plan for?" Don't take the answer as gospel. No one can possibly predict the weather months ahead. If you can't stand cold or wetness, pack what you need to combat those possibilities, even if you're going into the desert in August. Just don't overdo anything.

10. "Are there facilities for cutting and wrapping meat available?" This and a properly cared for cape (the skin over the animal's neck and shoulders, which needs to be kept in good condition if you will later mount the head) should rate high on your list of "need to know" items.

What an outfitter can or cannot do is often a point of contention, both during and after a guided hunt. To clear up some common misconceptions, here are a few insights:

1. The guide or outfitter cannot guarantee, nor promise, a successful hunt for any trophy. The only exception to this is in the case of a private game preserve hunting situation which we shall not discuss here. Any outfitter who makes such promises is not a legitimate concern, and should be avoided like the plague. The only way that a guide could come through on such a promise is if he shot your animal for you—a completely illegal and unethical happening in any case. Should you ever find yourself in a situation where such a practice is offered or observed, *do not* become party to it. It takes only one law-abiding hunter or one disgruntled employee to drop a note to the Game and Fish Department, or phone a game warden with the information, and there goes not only the price of another hunt, but your hunting privileges as well. Having spoken your displeasure at the action, or suggestion, bide your time, and report it to the proper authorities when you get out of the camp.

2. Guides and outfitters cannot predict, nor control, the weather, hunting pressure, past winters, or the game's preference for a given location at a given time. What is a prime elk range in October with normal snowfall can be barren during an unusually dry fall.

3. Guides *can* know the area and the prime habitat resources in the hunt area. They can try to please your desires, and they can provide a clean, well-run camp and an ethical hunt. They can put you into regions not overrun with other hunters, and they can hunt as hard as you are willing to yourself.

It is not at all unusual for many first-time horseback hunters to fully expect to ride into the center of a herd of elk, calmly pick the lead bull from the mass of grazing bodies, and after one well-placed shot, watch the monarch drop in the alpine meadow. In reality, you may do this once in a great while, but it is not the rule. More likely, you'll ride into elk country and then hunt for the beasts on foot as you do anywhere else. If that is the offering, and it is not what you want, get it straight at the onset of the booking. Communication is the key. By the same token, if you can just barely handle riding five miles on horseback at a walk, don't book a hunt with a man who believes in camping five miles from the area and galloping full tilt to the hunting grounds before first light.

Should worse come to worst, and you end up in a bad situation despite your planning, don't sit back and say nothing. Another thing a guide can't do is read your mind. Make your feelings known in a pleasant, open manner.

I recall the experience of two American hunters in one of the Canadian provinces, where they had booked a moose hunt with a local outfitter. They were completely satisfied with everything provided, except the hunting method employed by the guide. This guide believed that the way to hunt moose was to ride from sunup to sundown and hope to see a moose feeding in the marshes. It soon became clear to them that the moose were not waiting around in the open once the horses appeared on the trails. Having had no opportunity for even a snapshot using this approach, they were ready to go home empty-handed. Finally, with only one day left to hunt, sore to the bone, the two hunters demanded that they be allowed to stop and glass each opening as they approached it. As a result, they killed one bull between them. Had they spoken sooner, there is every reason to assume that two moose may have been exported from that Canadian hunt to the United States that year.

It is of prime importance that you, as the client, offer certain information to the outfitter and guide prior to your arrival, and restate it once in camp. If you have any physical limitations, especially life-threatening ones, such as heart disease, diabetes, or diet restrictions, or special needs, let them know before you're up on the mountain with nothing but the clothes on your back. Don't assume that anyone else knows the correct way to deal with your condition. If you carry nitroglycerin tablets, show the others in camp how to administer them. If you have insulin, explain the difference between its need versus the need for added sugar in case of insulin shock at certain times. Don't try to get by on normal camp foods just because you don't want to burden the cook. Tell him what you can and can't have when you book the hunt so a menu can be planned accordingly. If you have diet restrictions, remind the cook again when you arrive in camp. If you are allergic to wool, let the outfitter know that so you don't end up with a surplus wool army blanket under your saddle. The old adage, "better safe than sorry," applies twice over in the wilderness.

Don't expect a refund of your deposit if you cancel out on a booked hunt. After all, the outfitter has a massive amount of money tied up in an enterprise that lasts only a few months out of every twelve. If you don't show up, there is a real chance that no one else will be able to fill the gap. This is becoming more and more the case as many states now limit license availability to computer-drawn permits instead of selling them as over-the-counter commodities.

Try to understand that the average saddle horse costs $500 or more, and requires year-round maintenance. Tack is a real bargain at $400 a set, and the staff gets paid the same whether there is one hunter or nine in camp. Then there are the other cost factors: food, camp costs, license fees, mechanical transportation, and not least, the man's profit margin. Therefore, before you book a hunt, and plop down one-third or one-half of a multi-hundred-dollar fee, be damn sure you're going to show up! The only two exceptions are when booking through an agency which guarantees refunds, or when you cancel early enough to allow the spot to be filled by another hunter.

Your attitude may contribute immensely to the success or failure of your hunt. I'll tell you a story that will show you what I mean.

Bob is 35 years old, and is an executive with a major company. While good at giving orders, he has little need for tact in his day-to-day life. He has hunted since he was old enough to tag along, and living in Pennsylvania, he has taken his share of whitetails. He booked his first guided hunt with Outfitter A in northwest Wyoming. Bob asked, and was told, that the outfitter would supply all but personal items for the hunt. At that point, Bob stopped asking questions and departed for the hunt with his rifle, ammunition, toothbrush, and clothes. He was met at the airport by the outfitter, and driven to the base camp on the mountain. He was shown a wall tent complete with cots, and was told that this would be home for the next ten days. His initial reaction was that it looked awfully barren, and where were the sleeping bags? The answer? "They are personal equipment!"

Bob was outraged, and he let everyone know about it in short order. The outfitter calmed his client and told Bob he would bring an extra sleeping bag for him. That night, as the evening meal was being prepared, the camp cook asked Bob to get a pail of water from the storage tank. Bob responded that he was not getting paid to carry water for the hired help, and this set the tone for his next thirty meals.

During supper, Bob told his guide that he knew everything there was to know about hunting. After all, he was a successful whitetail hunter, and nothing was smarter than a whitetail buck! From that point on, all the information that the guide, who had twenty years of experience, had been prepared to share was politely withheld from Mr. Know-it-all.

The next morning, Bob informed his guide on several occasions that the glassing of barren ridges they were doing was a waste of time. He was completely convinced that no buck of the stature he sought would be laying in such an exposed location. The guide tried to explain the difference between whitetails and mule deer, to no avail.

At his own insistence, during the course of the next few days, Bob found himself riding behind his silent guide to a spot overlooking a creek bed where he was dropped off, and left to sit alone, waiting for his trophy to wander by. By the ninth day, he had seen only a few does and fawns. That night, he dogged his guide for the buck he came after. Still unwilling to admit that he didn't know everything, he ranted and raved about the rip-off he was being handed.

Still silent, the guide led Bob to the rim of a canyon the next morning. Dismounting some distance away, he crept with the obnoxious hunter to the edge, and after a few moments of scanning with his binoculars, showed the man a three-point buck still in its bed. Bob made the shot and departed the camp that afternoon. No one was sorry to see him go, nor did they care if he ever came back.

Dave, on the other hand, is also 35. He too is an executive accustomed to giving orders. Being from New York, Dave has also taken a number of whitetails over the years. He arrived at the same airport, and was met by Outfitter A and driven to the mountain base camp Bob had just departed. Dave had everything he needed with him, since he had carried on a year-long letter and phone correspondence with the outfitter. At his request the outfitter had sent him a list of suggested items.

Once in camp, Dave pitched in and helped with carrying firewood, feeding the animals, and preparing the food. At supper, he asked to be shown his horse and the tack he'd use for the coming hunt, and inquired into the best methods to employ. The guide was pleasantly surprised to find an experienced hunter willing to ask questions and listen to the answers, and he spent hours around the campfire explaining options. By the time they turned in, Dave knew exactly what to expect come dawn.

After only two days of a seven-day hunt, Dave had a beautiful four-point buck hanging from the game pole. The antler beams were thick at the base, dark mahogany in color, with well-matched, ivory-tipped tines. He shot it within spittin' distance of where Bob had sat alone for hours the previous week. The only difference was that the guide, eager to help a friendly client, had ridden up through the willow-choked creek bottom and spooked the buck from his well-hidden bed.

The rest of Dave's hunt became a fishing and sight-seeing trip, adding greatly to the memories that he returned with to New York.

Today, Bob stares at the small three-point rack on his den wall, curses the outfitter, the guide, the cook, and the luck of his hunt. Dave looks at the magnificent four-point head mount with the twenty-eight-inch spread and feels a warm kinship with those same people. He sends and receives a Christmas card each year, and always enclosed in his card he finds the opening dates and prices for the next year's hunts, along with an invitation to again join the boys on the mountain.

Obviously, it was not a planned rip-off, nor ineffective guiding, cooking, or bad luck that ruined Bob's dream hunt. It was Bob's own attitude and lack of communication. It is hoped that we can all be Daves every time our turn comes to "join the boys on the mountain."

Another story will illustrate the need to check out any professional prior to making a deposit and booking the hunt. Several years ago, I was asked to guide for a new out-fitter in western Wyoming. That outfitter wanted to hire me over the phone, having never spoken to me prior to the offer. He didn't know if I would be assigned to a horseback hunt in the mountains (in an area I had never seen before), or to an antelope camp 150 miles from my home (also an area I had no first-hand knowledge of). I did not guide for that outfitter, because I could not have done justice to any hunters delivered into my hands. I sometimes wish that I had done so, however, for I can't imagine the kind of hunt they must have had in the company of the "guides" who ultimately did accept the jobs under those conditions.

Again, the very first place to start is with the Game and Fish Department of the state in which the outfitter works. If the outfitter is licensed, proceed to check the references he has supplied. If he is not licensed, cross him off your list and pick another firm.

Another option, open to at least some hunters, is to hunt with a friend who lives in the area to be hunted. These resi-dent sportsmen are often as knowledgeable and able as the paid guides and outfitters, sometimes even more so. If you happen to fall into this category of fortunate hunters, there are some rules of etiquette to follow here as well.

One of the first things to bear in mind is that your sched-ule may not coincide with your friend's in terms of vacation time, family plans, or hunting areas. If indeed you ask, or are invited, to hunt with a resident friend, try to plan around his schedule, not yours. Just because he agrees to take you hunting with him does not mean that he does not wish to hunt himself. Also, your share of the expenses should not stop when you get to the friend's house. It may well be that if you were not there it would still cost the same amount for the friend to drive to the hunting area, feed the horses, and pay for food. But, bear in mind that *you* are getting the benefit of all those items, not the friend's spouse, son, daughter, or workmate who might have gone along if you had not been there. Offer to pay at least your share of the expenses, if not more. It will still cost you a lot less than the same hunt with a professional outfitter.

Next, just because that friend offers to take you hunting, don't assume, or even ask, if the invitation extends to your relatives and other friends. If it did, that situation would be made clear by the offering party. The point of the offer is usually to share an enjoyable time with you. The offer is not meant to make you out to be Diamond Jim Brady, who can take friends and business associates on a hunt for little or no cost to them.

I remember the time that one of my friends called to ask if I would take him hunting mule deer near my home in Wyoming. Having not seen him in nearly ten years, I was truly delighted at the prospect. Even when it became known that four other mutual friends from the past were planning to come along, I was not upset. Then, as the plans progressed, a phone call informed me that there was also to be another man who I did not know and three of his personal friends coming along, bringing the total number to nine. This was definitely getting out of hand! Out of respect for the friendship, and perhaps with some lack of intestinal fortitude, I said nothing.

The crux of the problem came to light months later when the original five hunters did not draw hunting permits, but the other four, who I did not know, did. Now, I had four hunters to escort into the mountains, only one of which

I had ever met before.

As things turned out, the situation only got worse. These men expected me to drive one hundred miles a day, provide my own food and gas, guide them to bucks, and in the end, shoot their animals for them. The experience left a rather bitter taste in everyone's mouth when it was over. I felt used and obligated, especially since I had already filled my tag, and I am fairly sure they felt let down and abandoned.

Considering that experience, I seldom invite anyone to hunt with me, and if I do, I tend to be quite frank about who is invited, how the costs are borne, and how many hunters will be considered. I refuse to ever again pay for the privilege of helping out a group of strangers.

I am not trying to dissuade you from attempting to hunt with a true friend. It should be clear to you, however, that to take advantage of a friendship is a sure way to lose a portion of it forever. You are the controlling factor in most of these situations—make them enjoyable and rewarding, not harmful and destructive. Through communication, planning, and respect for guides and hunting partners, you can ensure your chances for a successful and enjoyable horseback hunt.

Chapter 3

Gear & Clothing

The clothing and gear that accompany you on a horse-back hunt can make or break the trip in short order. Before you can know what to pack, you have to know where you're going to be hunting and seasonal variations in weather conditions.

For an early hunt on the high plains or desert after mule deer, you won't go far dressing like an extra in a 1880s Western movie. The typical cowboy hat is just fine on the open range where it acts as sun visor and rain deflector in one. But for the hat to be of service, rather than a pain in the neck, it must fit! Too loose and the wind will ship it to the next county in no time. Too tight and you'll suffer some whiz-bang headaches. A chin strap is not a bad thing on a hunting hat. This string allows you to tip the hat off, for added cooling or while glassing for game, without having to hang onto it with one hand.

In direct contrast to the open lands, forested mountains do not lend themselves well to the wearing of a Western hat. Tree branches will alternately snatch the sombrero off your head, or play little tunes on the brim as the felt acts like a sounding board for every leaf and twig. In addition to game-alerting sounds and the agony of dismounting to recover the misplaced headgear, your ears will change color from pink to purple when the temperature drops and the wind howls.

A much better choice for cold, mountain hunting is a visored winter cap with built-in earflaps. A well-constructed stocking cap will also do, but besides not having a sun-shielding visor, this type of hat suffers even more from the same affliction as do Western hats in that the tree limbs find the tiny knitting holes and lift the hat from your head to wave as trophies in the wind.

While we are on the topic of wind and cold, anyone who has suffered the effects of subzero temperatures on his lungs will understand the function of a bandanna. By wearing a bandanna of the traditional Western variety, or a scarf or ski mask, you can avoid the painful and sometimes deadly result of breathing extremely cold air. At the same time that a face cover is insulating the lungs, it also protects the external features from the abrasion of wind-powered ice crystals and grains of sand. Without this protection, such minute projectiles can turn your skin into something akin to hamburger in a few hours—or less.

Because of the dry air and nearly constant wind in the West, one item to throw in your pocket for sure is lip balm. Chapstick can become a commodity as precious as gold when your lips begin to crack open twenty miles from the nearest road.

Boots, like hats, should change with terrain and season. On the plains in early fall, Western boots are hard to beat for comfort in the saddle. The problem comes when you have to get out of the saddle and try to negotiate a six-degree slope covered by shale or loose rock. Then those same boots become a detriment to the wearer. When the thermometer drops and snow falls, plain Western boots are about as useful as old newspapers. At those times, you would probably consider selling your soul for a pair of waterproof, insulated, lace-up hunting boots. But be careful here, as flat, Vibram-type soles with slight heels are a real hazard in a stirrup. If your foot ever slips through, it'll be hell getting it out. For this same reason, tennis shoes, running shoes, and other flat-bottomed soles and boots are not great for riding. The best solutions I've come across so far are insulated Western-style boots, or something equally warm and waterproof with a substantial heel.

A standard stirrup is shown placed inside an oversized stirrup for comparison.

While you're thinking about boots, bear in mind that some sizes and designs may not fit into a standard stirrup. Prior to departing for your hunt, check to see if the boots you intend to wear do fit a normal stirrup. If indeed they do not, ask your outfitter if he has oversized stirrups on his saddles. If the answer is no, buy a set. You simply cannot force an oversized shoe into an undersized stirrup. If you can't get your foot in the thing, you can't mount, ride, or hunt in comfort or safety.

Lest you think that chaps are simply something "cute" to keep your jeans clean, let me enlighten you a bit. When the day comes that you are introduced to greasewood, you will change your opinion. Greasewood is a type of shrub that looks like sagebrush, or, perhaps easier to relate to, a large, finely branched cactus. In any case, it has some of the most piercing thorns that ever broke off in your hide. Worse than that, they don't stop with just the hide. I've had half-inch greasewood thorns buried so deep in my thigh muscles that they had to be cut out with a scalpel. The price of chaps looked like a real bargain after that experience.

In addition to protecting you from penetration by alien flora, chaps serve another function. If you have ever sat in a saddle during a snowstorm, or had a heavy, wet accumulation of the white stuff fall in your lap from the treetops, you know how your legs are soon soaked to the skin. With a set of good chaps on, your legs will stay as dry as the inside of a tent. Unlike some gear, chaps are not a "must have" item, but they certainly are not useless weight, either.

Gloves are like boots and hats—the kind you use depends on where and when you use them. Insulated gloves are needed in the cold, but on the desert, a pair of unlined leather gloves is far superior. Do you think you don't need gloves if it isn't cold? Try letting a horse jerk a rope or set of reins through your clenched fist and see if those pretty white burns are worth the lack of protection.

As in any situation, several layers of clothes which can be put on or removed as needed, without greatly increasing or decreasing your body temperature, are preferable to one or two heavy items of apparel. Pack a couple sets of light-weight, insulated underwear. The two-piece style takes better advantage of the layering principle. The heavy quilted stuff is just too thick and bulky to be of much use. One set of insulated coveralls go with me on any hunt, even in the desert. They feel mighty good before dawn breaks.

One thing to avoid on a horseback hunt is any garment, worn below the waist, that has a heavy seam or reinforced overlaps in the seat area. It takes very little time for these tiny eruptions to crater your buttocks in a saddle.

Another thing for you to leave at home is a set of spurs. For one thing, you won't need them. Beyond that, they are noisy, and if you don't know how to ride well, dangerous. The natural inclination for the tyro when a horse gets going too fast or acts up in some way is to squeeze the feet tighter

Spurs are best left hanging on the wall at home during a hunt, if you don't know how to wear them.

against the animal. When you squeeze with spurs on, you'll get a real ride! Forget about the romantic image and leave them hanging on the wall.

For those of you who do not already have to wear prescription eyeglasses, or who do not have photogray lenses, a good set of sunglasses is another required item. Snow blindness is a painful experience, and the same condition can occur when the sun reflects from alkali flats or desert sand. The small amount of space and infinitesimal weight is well spent on this protective equipment.

Well, we have you pretty well dressed now, at least to the point where you can finish by yourself. Let me just say one more thing about outer clothing. Though well known, this fact seems to be overlooked, or forgotten: wool is both silent and warm, both wet and dry. If you are allergic to wool, chamois is close to it for silence.

Now let's turn our attention to the equipment that goes

with a horseback hunt. Make sure you have the following items in your personal saddle gear: canteen, compass, binoculars, saddlebags, scabbard, lock-blade pocket knife with sharpener, and compact first-aid kit. A rubberized poncho or long-tailed raincoat will keep you, your saddle, and your saddlebags dry.

Everyone has his own preference in canteens, so my only advice is that you carry as many quart-size canteens and purification tablets as necessary according to your water situation and length of hunt. If you intend to carry a canteen on the saddle using the shoulder strap, I suggest that you will want to replace or reinforce the factory-supplied strap. The first few times a canteen filled with a quart of water bounces up and down, most flimsy cotton straps snap. Heavy canvas webbing or nylon cords that extend around the base of the canteen cover and support it from below are best.

At this time, you should also use electrical tape to cover all chains, buckles, and other metal noisemakers. Remember that left unattended, these tinkling items become an eight-piece band as a horse walks along.

The binoculars are best kept in the saddlebags, their own carrying case on the saddle, or in your pocket. The best bet is to own the newer compact type that is about the size of a pack of cigarettes. These binoculars will fit in a pocket and be there ready to use when you need them. The old trick of hanging the binoculars around your neck and tucking them inside a shirt or jacket is fine until the horse starts to trot. At that point, the last thing you'll want is half a pound of anything solid ricocheting off of your chest. For the same reason, a rifle slung on your back is not recommended on horseback.

Without starting a major argument, let me suggest that a lock-blade pocket knife with a three- or four-inch blade can do any job a sheath knife can, and takes up less room. If you want to drag along a bayonet, it's okay with me, but you don't need it.

Saddlebags are a great asset on a hunt. They can hold maps, sandwiches, extra ammunition, canteens, rope, rain

Compact binoculars are a real asset on a horseback hunt. (Photo courtesy of Michaels of Oregon)

jackets, and extra clothes that you discard as the day warms up, or put on as it cools down. They are also an excellent place for the first-aid kit, flashlight, snacks, extra matches or smoking materials, and, if you have to quarter an animal, such helpful tools as a hatchet and saw of the belt variety. When buying or borrowing saddlebags, forget anything made of thin canvas, plastic, or synthetic leatherette. Such "economy" models seldom last long enough to make it to base camp. Get a reinforced nylon or heavy leather set and they will still be hanging on a saddle when your grandkids are riding.

The same admonition holds true for any other gear you might pick up. Vinyl or plastic material for tarps, rain gear, and other items is noisy, breaks when frozen or moved in the cold, and in general, is unsuitable for use. Also, make sure that the design of the saddlebags allows for completely secure closures, not only on the front of the bag, but on the sides as well. If you get a set that bows out on the top corners, everything will bounce out of those gaping maws in a few miles.

What to put in your first-aid kit is another question which can start an ongoing argument that can last the winter and

Binocular cases should have a strong nylon or leather strap supporting the case from below for saddle use. (Photo courtesy of Bushnell, division of Bausch & Lomb)

half the spring without being agreed upon. Suffice it to say that if you need it at all, you probably need it very badly. For that reason alone, it should contain the items needed to save a life, not just cover a scratch.

Now, a brief word about your weapons and ammo. With your rifle, you should consider taking your own scabbard, tailored for the weapon. Trying to fit a bolt-action rifle equipped with a scope into a scabbard made for a carbine is tantamount to stuffing a size-twelve foot into a size-six loafer. In the event that you choose to buy a scabbard for the occasion, get one that not only fits your rifle, but also has a hood. Failing that, a set of scope covers is a must. Snow and rain accumulate in a scabbard like bats in a cave. Last, if you have no hood for your scabbard, be sure that it has a retaining strap of some kind. Despite Hollywood's depictions, rifles in boots attached to horses are not very secure. It is not at all uncommon to lose a rifle from an open boot.

I think I just heard someone out there say, "What about a pistol?" To that I say, it's your party. If you want to bring a handgun, and it's legal in the area, do so. If not, that's okay too. Having been left without a rifle by an errant horse from time to time, I always carry one. For that purpose, you may as well carry something in the .44 Magnum category that will legally take the game you're after. I'll tell you another secret that isn't in the movie scripts: the purpose of the leg tie-down thong on a pistol holster was not for fast draws; it was to keep the leather in place as the horse galloped! Without some secure anchor like this, the holster usually ends up in your armpit.

Of course, you need a sleeping bag, and either an air mattress or a pad. Here, too, you should not scrimp on quality. A plain cotton or flannel bag will feel like cheesecloth in the middle of the night. A cheap mattress will be full of holes before the trip is over. Get a good, subzero bag filled with down or fiberfill. The pad or mattress adds insulation as well as cushions. Choose all of your gear carefully.

A small flashlight is a must, as is a propane lighter or waterproof matches. In addition to your personal toilet arti-

Sleeping bags should be compact and of high quality for a horseback trip. (Photo courtesy of Coleman Products)

Scope covers are a must during rain or snowfall. (Photo courtesy of Michaels of Oregon)

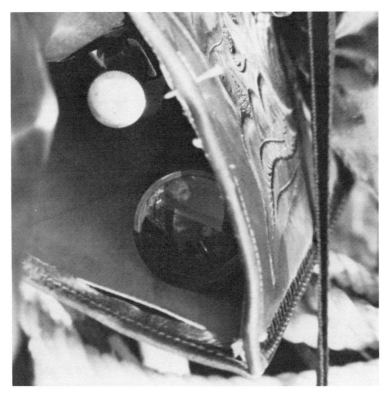

An unhooded scabbard is a great collector of dirt and snow.

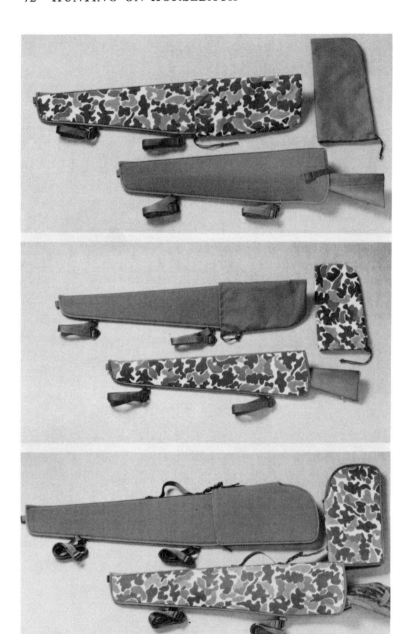

A retaining strap prevents your rifle from slipping, or from being pulled from rear-mounted scabbards. (Photo courtesy of Michaels of Oregon)

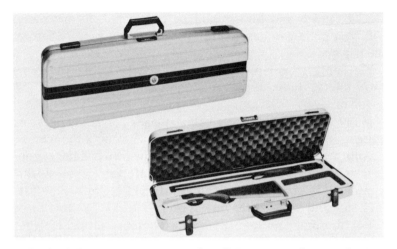

A hard-sided gun case is a must when flying to your hunting destination. (Photo courtesy of Sturm, Ruger & Company)

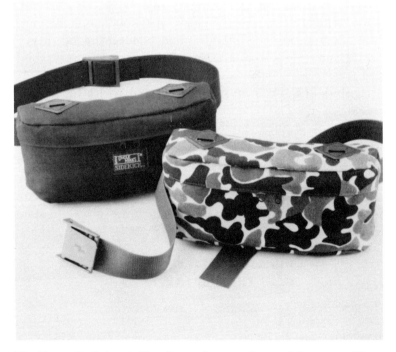

The Fanny Pack is considered superior to a day pack by some. (Photo courtesy of Michaels of Oregon)

cles, a camera and film should be considered. I'll bet there will be a million dollars worth of memories to capture before the trip ends.

Not only to comply with most state laws, but for your own safety, outer wear of fluorescent orange should be included.

Many folks find that a small day-pack, or fanny-pack, is quite useful on the hunt. Not a requirement, but a thought.

Another possible consideration is your own saddle. If you have a saddle which you consider comfortable, you might want to take it with you. Many outfitters get by with what they can, and some of the tack is pretty "tacky."

For those of you taking your own horses hunting, remember to throw in a set of shoes, nails, and a multipurpose shoeing tool. Sure as you're born, the ornery cuss will throw a shoe in the hinterland. You have to be able to replace it, or pull them all. In like manner, take along the necessary items to tend to veterinary needs of the animal in the outback. In addition to antiseptic and bandages, good, heavy needle and thread for stitching major cuts is a very good idea.

Hobbles are also a must if you intend to let the animal forage for itself. Many horses soon learn to make a good many miles in these hoof-cuffs, however, so don't expect your horse to remain in a thirty-foot area without an inducement such as a morning grain ration, which means we've added feed to the take-along list.

The checklists that follow are not intended to be complete lists of every item needed. Rather, they are places to start getting ready.

CHECKLIST OF GEAR FOR A
GUIDED HUNT

Clothes

Bandanna/scarf/face mask
Boots
Gloves

Miscellaneous

Camera and film
Canteen and purification
 tablets

Handkerchiefs
Hat/cap
Insulated coveralls
Long underwear
Rain gear
Shirts
Socks
Trousers

First-aid kit
Mattress/pad
Moccasins
Personal medication
Sleeping bag
Snacks/drinks
Soap
Toilet paper
Toothbrush
Towel and washcloth

Hunting Equipment

Binoculars
Compass
Flashlight
Fluorescent orange items
Hunter's saw/hatchet
Hunting license
Knife and sharpener
Maps
Saddlebags/day pack
Scabbard
Scope covers
Sling
Sunglasses/eyeglasses
Weapons and ammunition

CHECKLIST OF ADDITIONAL GEAR IF BRINGING YOUR OWN HORSES

Blankets
Bridles
Camp gear
Feed
Halter
Hobbles
Horse shoes
Lariat

Lead ropes
Multipurpose tool
Nails
Pack saddle
Panniers
Ropes
Saddles
Veterinary supplies

Chapter 4
Planning Your Trip

Planning is the key to any successful trophy hunt. One way you may simplify the planning process is to work through a booking agent who specializes in hunting trips. One such agency that serves as an example is Jack Atcheson & Sons, Inc., of Butte, Montana. Not only will such an agency make available a selection of guides and outfitters who offer the game you wish to pursue in the geographic area you intend to hunt, but it will represent you if you have a bad experience with any client to whom it referred you. In addition to this plus, hunting trip agencies operate under the same principle as do travel agents, getting their fees from the outfitters, not from you. They are an exceptional bargain and well worth investigation.

Even when the outfitter or booking agent arranges for the license, permits, and transportation, there are still many things for you to consider. Not the least of these is the manner in which you are traveling to and from any major transportation system. Having the airline reservations made for you is one thing. But finding out on the day of departure that, due to road construction, a normal one-hour drive is now two extra hours worth of waiting could be a rude awakening and could shave hours or days off your time in the saddle. Spending good money for a hard-sided gun case to meet airline requirements is great until you show up at the boarding desk and are informed that only metal cases are accepted by that particular carrier, while yours is made of plastic. Of such little quirks are spoiled trips made!

I know of few better ways to show you what Lady Luck and lack of planning can do to a trip than to tell you yet another story that took place many years ago. The following narrative is the true tale of the rigors one must face, and the trials and tribulations one must overcome, before, during, and after the hunt.

It all started more than a year before the actual departure. An advertisement in the back of an outdoor magazine caught my eye. "Hunt Wild Boar in Tennessee!" it proclaimed. It struck a nerve, kind of how that last piece of pie awaiting you in the refrigerator preys on your mind. So, during a horseback elk hunt near my Wyoming home, over the course of breakfast, lunch, and supper, not to mention while he was trying to sleep or occupied in the latrine, I casually mentioned to my lifelong friend, Ken Rice, that we ought to consider a pig hunt. After several days and nights of this, Ken gave in and agreed to make the hunt a joint endeavor. I am fairly certain after looking back on it, that the major reason he did so was out of concern for my personal safety, for I'm sure he was ready to strangle me. He, however, maintains that it was in the hopes of preserving his own sanity. At any rate, the wheels were set in motion.

After many letters and several phone calls, the deposits were in the mail. Airline tickets were waiting at the travel agent's office and our gear began to find its way into the duffle bags. We now waited in earnest for H-hour to arrive (H is for hunt).

Never one to pass up a chance to be left in peace and quiet, Ken suggested I call a mutual friend in Minnesota and invite him to meet us in Tennessee, thereby giving me a new victim to harangue. It took only a short time for Bernie Szezesniak to persuade two of his buddies, Rod and "Bozo," to also make the trek. Now the stage was really set. Five veterans of whitetail, mule deer, elk, and bear hunts were going to pit their knowledge, skill, and courage against the untamed fury of wild hogs! It just had to be a hunt to remember.

Ken and I met in Laramie. Loading my gear into his pick-up, we drove to Denver where we were to catch our flight to Chattanooga, Tennessee. While it seemed like six, we had only a one-hour delay in our flight's departure time. Without incident, we landed in Tennessee and proceeded to rent a car for the drive to the hunting preserve. We did not choose the "Number One" agency to rent the car from; suffice it to say that it was a minor competitor. Having been twenty-four hours without sleep by this time, we got a motel room and slept for about five hours. Now rested and in high spirits, we had a meal of pork chops (what else?) and headed for the hunting camp.

The first big thrill of the trip now came. With a full day and a night to waste before meeting the frenzied boar on its home turf, we stopped to pick up a little libation. It was Sunday. Has anyone out there ever heard of something called a Blue Law? No booze!

Thirty miles from our destination, our attention was drawn to a strange and unexplainable sight. There, in the middle of the Tennessee woods, was a traffic light. It was red, of course. At that mysteriously placed stoplight were two cars, both of them headed in the same direction. Our rental was first in line; the other vehicle directly behind us bore Minnesota license plates. Inside could be noted three jowly (all hog hunters are jowly) faces peering intently at the two cowboy hats in the car ahead of them. It was our friends. Obviously, the hand that had placed the traffic light at this desolate intersection had also guided our hunting compan-ions and us, from separate origins a thousand miles apart, to this spot at precisely the same moment.

Arriving at the hunting preserve, which shall remain name-less, we introduced ourselves and were assigned our quarters. After settling in, we all proceeded to the firing range to make certain that our wide assortment of weapons still held their zero. After all our rifles, pistols, and revolvers had been tested, we now felt ready to do battle with the ferocious swine which we all knew, from reading tons of swine literature, awaited us in the wooded hills. I can't swear to it, but I tend to believe that while we were there, Bernie may have sighted in his knife! Such was the high state of anticipation within the group.

Having been told by our host, who reminded us of a modern-day Rhett Butler, that we would be off "bright and early," we retired with the sun, and arose well before dawn. At first light, we were raring to go. At second light, we were still raring, but so far, we hadn't gone anywhere. Apparently, in Tennessee, "bright" comes about nine o'clock, and "early" comes around an hour later. By 10 a.m., our host was regaling the group with a lecture on the biological, physiological, and psychological makeup of our adversary. By the time he had finished, only a great white shark seemed a more deadly foe.

Following that bit of propaganda, we were loaded onto pickup trucks which hauled us to the hills. In the company of ten other neophyte hog hunters, all armed to the teeth and willing to do battle with Beelzebub himself by this time, we were marched into the hardwood-covered hills by the guides.

Once in the woods, we were broken into two parties. Having been chosen to "man the line," I and several others were spread out at intervals resembling a full division prepared to repulse attacking hordes of tanks. We sat there for an hour and a half. No one on the line saw a living organism larger than a microbe. The two "recon" patrols did sight the quarry, and one little porker bit the dust, albeit without a tusk being bared. Probably the lack of ivory was because the wiry little fellow had not reached puberty, much less maturity.

Having survived this first engagement without a casualty, we were given orders to advance to the rear. Withdrawing to the camp, we had lunch, having no doubt burned up maybe fifteen or twenty calories each in our morning excursions. Most of the assembled company were long-time hunters like ourselves, and there were few happy faces when the ranks formed up for the next maneuver.

It was 1400 hours by then, and the Commander surveyed his troops with a stern eye as he promised them that things would now be different. The secret weapon was about to be unleashed on the enemy. It was indeed different from the rather short morning, but hunting with the pack of dogs was not necessarily any better. In two hours, the hounds had run pigs to everyone. You could literally have stuck some with a knife, and fifteen dead hogs hung from the meat pole!

We did our best to make it a hunt. We turned down hogs, we went to the dogs instead of waiting for them to run a herd past us, we even waded into the battles between the dogs and hogs. Our group of five hunters ended up with three of the top tuskers taken that day. Mine was one of them, so you can see that it is not sour grapes when I say that this wasn't our kind of hunting. If we had talked to someone who had been there before, we would have saved ourselves a lot of disappointment.

With the hunting completely over in only three and one-half hours, we still had another full day to kill before our flight home.

The next morning, having said their goodbyes, the boys from Minnesota drove off and left Ken and I to the task of organizing our quartered meat and the salted capes for the return flight. All of this perishable "baggage" we carefully packed into three large GI duffle bags lined with plastic, and then iced it all down. Each bag, thus filled, held well over 100 pounds. These bags were kept fresh in the camp's electric cooler until departure time arrived.

Ken allowed as how we ought to leave a little early, in case we had a flat tire on the way to the airport. Not one to cause undue stress, I didn't mention the fact that while packing gear into the trunk of the rented car, I had noticed that it was devoid not only of a spare tire, but of jack, lug wrench, and tools of any kind. There was a small bracket meant for a can of instant tire—fix-a-flat—but it, too, was empty.

Arriving at the airport, about two quarts low on sweat, I returned the rented car. My remarks about "Number One" having spare tires apparently went unnoticed in the rush to collect the fee. At the check-in counter, Ken greeted me with the same slanted glance that I've learned to hate seeing since our days together in first grade. The airline didn't accept any bag weighing more than sixty-five pounds!

I have often wondered since that fateful day, just how many calls the Chattanooga Police received from the airport. Probably the initial five or six reports of two wild-eyed maniacs, transferring bloody corpse parts from GI duffle bags into plastic-lined, cardboard boxes in the men's room of the airport terminal (which was the only place available for such delicate work), all the time screaming obscenities about weak-backed, chicken-hearted baggage handlers, were chalked up to heatstroke victims. But, certainly the final, metal-rending, boot-scuffing raid on the uncooperative ice machine rated a cruise by at the very least.

Now re-packed, re-iced, and accepted as baggage, the raw pork slid from our sight on the conveyer belt. Just as the last box disappeared, the ticket clerk informed us of another unplanned development. Our flight to Denver was being routed through Atlanta, Georgia. There, we would have a three-hour layover, and the temperature was currently well over 100 degrees. I, for one, was quite relieved to learn that he was speaking of the Fahrenheit, and not the Celsius scale. His next bit of good news was this: "If the meat starts to spoil, you will be paged in the terminal and you will have to do something with it!"

Ken and I made a pact in pig blood right then and there. If our names were mentioned, even in casual conversation, we would very calmly get up and walk out of the Atlanta terminal and hitchhike to Wyoming.

After what were possibly the longest non-combat hours of our lives, our flight departed from Georgia enroute to Denver. Along with the usual notes of interest about our flight, such as our altitude, cruising speed, and points of interest on the route, the pilot mentioned in passing that the Denver airport was currently snowed in. With the thought of landing in Salt Lake City, Utah, with 300 pounds of rotting meat to contend with foremost in our minds, we flew merrily on. By some miracle, we became the first flight in nearly twenty-four hours to land in Denver. Now, all we had to do was collect our baggage and head north.

Ken was somewhat disheartened to find that his suitcase had split open on one end, exposing his skivvies to the world, and the very obvious fact that his rifle muzzle protruded from a newly worn hole in his gun case didn't do much to improve his outlook. He soon forgot these minor inconveniences, however, when I pointed out to him that one box of meat was missing completely. Spending two hours in a vain search for the errant box of meat did seem to set Ken on edge a bit. I, on the other hand, was in complete control of my emotions, merely threatening to eliminate the procreative ability of only two or three minor airline officials if they failed to help us find the missing box.

Having filled out all of the forms needed for lost baggage claims, and after waiting for Atlanta to call back to say they didn't have it, a very large, blue plastic bag sitting in the very center of the baggage claim area caught my eye. Perhaps the most striking thing about that bag was the way the pale blue contrasted so nicely with the bright red pool of pig blood in the center of which this bag proudly sat. We knew that it had not been there earlier, and we also knew that we had not used any blue plastic bags. Still, one look inside left no doubt, we had our meat back. The split cardboard indicated clearly that someone had dropped the box and then sat around trying to figure out what to do with fifty pounds of bloody meat and melting ice. The Denver PD would no doubt find out firsthand what the Chattanooga PD may have gone through several hours earlier. We, however, did not stay around to find out.

Packing all of the assorted parcels into Ken's truck, we were off! Almost.

Only one other thing needed to be done first. We had to go find a battery charger. Now, Ken is not one to leave things to chance, and his pickup had not one, but two 12-volt batteries under the hood. Unfortunately, both had decided to go on vacation when we did and it seemed we had beaten them back. Soon overcoming this slight impediment, we made it out of the parking lot. Thank goodness, only one of Ken's two gas tanks had a locking gas cap. Even though that one refused to respond to the key, we were able to fill the other tank with gas, and after battling for only five hours over 150 miles of black ice through a raging blizzard and freezing cold, made it home.

The meat had not spoiled, and it was excellent eating. As I write this, the mounted boar head glares at me from the wall reminding me for all time to plan, plan, plan! In addition, it keeps telling me that no amount of planning will alter fate, and we have to be flexible.

As you can see, there is a virtual panorama of things to consider before a departure date arrives. With the pressure on guides and outfitters what it is today, two years ahead of time is not too soon to start planning for this type of hunt. In fact, if you don't plan that far ahead, you will quite likely find that everything is booked, and you will have to start all over anyway.

The following is by no means a complete planning checklist, but each question needs to be addressed at some point. You can add to it, or delete from it, depending on the trip you have in mind.

1. Have you checked out the hunt to be sure it is what you think it is? If you have discussed the expectations and options with the outfitter, and if you have called and talked to people who have actually paid for and made the hunt you're going on, you've made a good start.

2. If you intend to hunt a new area without a guide, have you gotten all the information possible on the locale?

3. Where are you going? Geographic and seasonal variations make a big difference in terms of clothing and equipment required.

4. What are you going to hunt when you get there and what are you going to hunt with? Taking a .222 to shoot brown bear is equal to suicide.

5. How are you getting there and back? If you are driving

the full distance, is your vehicle up to the trip? If you are flying or taking other mass transport, have all commitments for paid services been finalized?

6. Is your vacation date scheduled at work to coincide with the trip dates? Are you actually scheduled to hunt on the dates you will be there? If your airline reservations are confirmed, is there a backup in case any flights get canceled, or are you leaving enough time in advance of your hunt to be able to lay over? Do you have a place to stay until the hunt starts?

7. How will you care for and transport meat and capes? The early seasons of August and September require more planning in terms of meat preservation because of the temperature extremes at those times. This is particularly important if you are driving, or have major layovers.

8. Have you considered the possible delays caused by inclement weather, or mechanical failure in your travel plans?

9. Do you have a taxidermist picked out? If so, will the outfitter ship to that person, or must you do so? This is one area that many people overlook. You should never entrust a trophy to the care of a taxidermist whose work you have not examined personally. Taxidermists must be artists. A poor one can ruin any mount, a good one can enhance any memory.

10. Will all the commercial forms of transportation that you will be using allow you to carry firearms? If not, how will you get your weapon to the hunt and back home? Though most airlines will carry firearms in hard-sided cases when they are unloaded and separate from the ammunition, some have policies against the practice. Some airlines only take metal cases, and some require their own labels. Some only accept weapons personally inspected by the airline personnel, or require the breakdown of the weapon. Pay particular attention to the smaller "short-hop" services that may connect between major flights—they often have strange regulations.

One solution to the weapon portion of the question is

not for the shoestring budget. Many hunters have found that the simplest answer, for them, is to buy a rifle at the hunt site and leave it as a tip for the guide when the hunt ends. Personally, I consider this highly unacceptable for many reasons, not the least of which is that you cannot have faith in a weapon you have owned for only a short time. Secondly, you may not find anything even close to what you want upon arrival in a strange place. Third, with the multitude of variable gun laws in different locations throughout the world, there is no guarantee that you will even be able to purchase the gun if you find one you like. Planning around restrictive transportation policies is far superior to this "easy out."

One possible solution is to have your gun shipped via United Parcel Service to a federal firearms licensed dealer near your hunt site. Don't try to cut corners here. It is illegal to ship a gun through the mails to other than a license holder. One must be careful to have good references on the dealer prior to such a practice. In this manner, you can be assured that your weapon is waiting for you when you arrive.

Now is also the time to check out the gear that you intend to take along on the trip. The embarrassment of wearing shirts with no buttons, or pants with the seat ripped out, is minimal compared to the discomfort and danger of finding yourself in the mountains with boots that have no soles, or a jacket whose lining is still in your closet. Like all things in life, equipment wears out with time and neglect. A tent that has served well for twenty years may gradually become a cheesecloth while securely packed away in storage. Check everything for function and operation before you leave home.

If you are not a regular shooter, be sure to check out the shells you intend to use. Ammunition lasts a long time, but can change in performance characteristics. For the uninformed, sighting in with one type or batch of ammo and then using a different one will usually result in a miss. If you are hunting with a given load, sight in with it and take only that type of ammunition with you. If you must change, resight the gun to the new load.

On the same general topic, don't fall prey to the trap of thinking that because you qualified on the rifle range in basic training some X-number of years ago, you can shoot. Like all skills, marksmanship takes constant practice to maintain.

This is also the time to fill any prescriptions and resupply any over-the-counter drugs that you cannot get along without.

It's important to address a topic I find difficult to address—borrowing. No matter what I borrow, it either breaks or baffles me in its use. Nevertheless, if you are going to borrow anything for the trip, get it ahead of time and test it out while learning to use it. If I had a dollar for every time that some nimrod confessed to me that he didn't know how to remove the safety from the rifle he'd borrowed, I wouldn't need to write for a living.

If you are taking along a partner to hunt with you and share costs, is that person someone you can get along with under any adversity?

If you look at all the nerve-wracking situations that arose on my trip to Tennessee, you will understand why this is a very important consideration. Ken and I could easily have taken our frustrations out on each other and ruined the trip totally. You can be guaranteed that in a twenty-four-hour drive, or a week's isolation in a hunting camp, every inter-personal conflict will be intensified tenfold. Because of this, any animosity between you and your companion will soon reach homicidal proportions.

I recall an antelope hunt in the Wyoming desert one year that illustrates the point further. Tom Gaddis and I had purposely packed a mobile camp so that we could sleep wherever the day ended instead of driving for miles after the sun went down. For some reason, unknown to me to this day, Tom absolutely refused to pitch camp anywhere except at our original camping spot. By day's end, this place was forty miles distant as the crow flies. Unfortunately, we didn't have a crow. After five hours and nearly 100 miles of driving in two states, we were back at our starting point. We weren't speaking to each other, but we were there. A few hours of sleep took away the tensions of the previous night, and we remain friends to this day. But if there had been any rift to begin with, that episode would have been the final straw. So, I say to you again, pick your partner with great care.

If your destination is outside the United States, be sure to have the proper documents required for the border crossings and any inoculations, and check the customs laws for contraband as defined by the destination country. For instance, Canada will not permit handguns of any type for any reason, and they limit the amount of ammunition you may bring in.

The same applies to horses. If you are hauling them out of your home country, or across state lines, be sure that you have brand inspection and health certificate papers that are up to date.

Remember always the silent admonition from the cold, staring eyes of my wild boar—plan, plan, plan! Then, expect to deal with a plan gone awry.

Chapter 5

Getting in Shape

A s with all sports, if you are not in shape for the task at hand, you will be miserable before the first day of a hard hunt is over. A horseback hunt can be extremely draining on several of the muscle groups. Nothing exactly matches the experience of sitting in a saddle all day long, and if you don't prepare for the coming ordeal, it will be just that, an ordeal.

You may have it in your mind that since the horse is going to do all of the work, there is no need for you to work out in preparation for the hunt. I'll go so far as to agree that a horseback hunt can be less strenuous on the heart and lungs than the same hunt might be on your own two legs. However, the new tension on your legs and back that comes with riding for hours will take its toll. By the end of an hour or two, you will feel like your knees and lower back are on fire. By the second day, your calves and thighs will have joined in the chorus of ouches and oofs. Rather than go through that pain during a once-in-a-lifetime hunt, get ready ahead of time and enjoy the experience when you actually saddle up for the real thing.

Nothing will replace daily rides on a live horse, but with additional exercises, you can help the various muscle groups ease into the regimentation. Before you set off on an exercise program of any kind, be it the material offered here or one of your own choosing, see your doctor and get his okay first. Suffering a heart attack by pushing a sedentary body too hard, too fast, is hardly a fine way to start the coming hunt.

While jogging is all the rage, there is little to show that it is really good for you. Quite the contrary, many physical problems are associated with the tremendous stress and concussion that occurs with this form of exercise. To many medical minds, the fast walk is as beneficial as hard running while having no ill effects. I suggest the fast walk as a good form of conditioning.

The following strengthening exercises can be done in your home or office with little room or special equipment required. Since the primary muscles used are in the legs and lower back, we will concentrate on those groups in the following sets.

The purpose of these exercises is twofold: they add strength to the muscles involved, and increase flexibility of the ligaments and joints. You will find both results of value when riding a horse. In all cases, the exercises must be done on the floor. The use of a bed, sofa, or other very moldable surface will make them useless. If the floor is too hard for you to be comfortable on, pad it with a quilt or heavy blanket. All the activities should be carried out at least ten times and repeated once or twice a day.

First read the instructions while studying the corresponding diagram, and then proceed.

Quad Sets

Lying on your back, or sitting with your back against a wall, begin with ten quad sets in each leg. With your legs straight, tighten the muscles on the front of your thigh, pulling the kneecap up as if to push the back of the knee into the floor. Hold the quadriceps in this "set" position for ten seconds, then relax the muscle group completely before repeating it.

Hamstring Sets

Still on your back, or sitting with your legs straight out, push your heels toward the floor, keeping the knee straight. When you feel the hamstring muscles on the back of your upper leg tighten, hold for ten seconds and again relax the muscle group completely before repeating.

Leg Lifts

To perform the straight leg raise, remain in the lying position and set the quad of one leg, then keeping the knee straight, lift that leg from the hip until it is about thirty inches off the floor at the heel. Hold for a ten count, then return the leg slowly to the floor. When you have finished ten with one leg, repeat with the other, or you may alternate. Do not brace your hands or arms against the floor to aid the lifts.

Knee Flex

Flexing the leg at the knee and hip, bring your knee as close as possible to your chest. It will increase your flexibility to reach up with your hands and pull the knee slightly closer to the chest after you have reached maximum flex with the muscles alone, but don't force too much. Return the leg to the starting position. Do ten with each leg.

Hip Abduction

Lying on your side, lift your top leg up and toward the rear, keeping the knee straight. When you reach the furthest point of hip abduction, hold for a five count and return to starting position. Do ten, then turn over and do the same with the opposite leg.

Chair-Assist Hip Adduction

Still on your side, place your uppermost leg on the seat of a chair placed in the normal position on its legs, with the front toward you. Using your top leg for leverage, lift the lower leg to the level of the chair seat. Hold for a five count and return to floor. After ten, turn over and repeat with the other leg.

Rear Leg Lift

Lying on your stomach, keep your knee straight and lift your leg from the hip toward the ceiling. At the furthest point you can attain, hold for a five count and return the leg to the floor. Do ten, then repeat with opposite leg.

Rear Knee Flex

While still on your stomach, bend your leg at the knee and flex your lower leg toward your buttocks as far as possible. Do ten flexes with each leg, returning to the starting position between each one. As with the knee to the chest flexing, pulling with your hand will increase the stretching action.

Hamstring Stretch

While sitting on the floor, keep the knees straight and place the legs in an open "V" position. Keep the feet as far apart as you possibly can and reach with both hands for one foot. Be sure to keep the knee straight and do not bounce. At the limit of your reach, hold the stretch for a five count, then relax. Repeat ten times for each leg.

Tiptoe Lift

In the standing position, place your hands on your hips, starting from a flat-footed stance, raise up on your tiptoes and hold for a ten count. Return to the flat-footed position and then back up on your toes. Continue this up-and-down routine at least ten times, and try to increase the number each day.

Finish up your workout with fifteen or twenty sit-ups and, by all means, try to find a horse to ride at least once a week in addition to the exercises.

We concluded earlier that a horseback hunt may be easier on the cardiovascular system than the same activity carried out walking. This statement holds true, but bear in mind the following two things: first, if you live in an area that is at or near sea level, the decrease in available oxygen at even a few thousand feet of altitude is going to be very noticeable. Second, you will not always be on the horse, and walking will still be an alternate method of locomotion. For those reasons alone, do not neglect the brisk walks, or some other pulse- and respiration-raising activity in your preparations.

In closing, remember that as much as we may wish it to be so, starting this program the week before departure will not achieve the desired results. Get to work!

Chapter 6
Camping

When you mention the word camping, people can conjure up all sorts of mental images. Some of them will be quite familiar to you; some you may not recognize at all. The term "camping" brings to mind that which you have been taught to believe it entails.

For some, it means a backpack, and very little else, under the stars. On the opposite side of the coin, some folks see a forty-foot motor home parked in a nicely manicured space on a concrete pad at a commercial camping area amidst 200,000 souls in the center of a major metropolitan area. When you say camping in conjunction with horseback, a good number of people see a chuck wagon, serenely resting on the prairie, with a herd of cows munching grass in the background. Add a few cowboys eating beans around the campfire and you have it.

In reality, camping is as diverse an activity as any of these images can portray it. The term "base camp" illustrates this to the greatest degree possible. When I hear the term, I think of the small group of tents or hard-sided campers parked in a meadow near the end of the last drivable road on the edge of a wilderness area. But then many affluent hunters feel that a base camp is that multi-million-dollar chalet from which to venture forth via truck, helicopter, or limousine to be transported into the hunting country in the morning. Then, at day's end, you are hauled back for a night of served dining, entertainment, and a rest between silk sheets.

If you can afford to book a hunt out of a chalet-type setting, you don't need to read my advice on the subject. So, let's confine our discussion to base camps and spike camps that are set up in the field by an outfitter or by yourself.

In a base camp run by a commercial outfitter, you can reasonably expect to find a comfortable setting including large wall tents containing stoves, beds in the form of cots, chairs and tables, lights in the form of gas lanterns, a cook, wranglers to handle stock which will usually be enclosed in a corral, plenty of fresh water, and possibly a portable shower arrangement. Your journey to that base camp will likely be in a motor vehicle and little or no limit will be imposed on what you bring along.

A spike camp, on the other hand, is little more than a shelter in the middle of hunting country, reached only by horseback, or by foot. It is used only for a night or so while seeking your quarry in its own backyard. There will be no luxuries, and even fresh water may be limited. Everything will have to come in with you on pack horses and therefore you will be extremely limited in what you can take along. The cooking may be done by the guide, or by you, as will the other chores, such as gathering and cutting wood, hauling water, and washing dishes.

Whenever the topic of spike camps comes up, I wish that my paternal ancestors were around to speak on the subject. If Uncle Jim or Uncle Charlie, my namesakes, were able to communicate with us, I am sure that we would learn a few things, for when they left Wisconsin and headed for Dakota Territory in the 1800s, they took only what they could stuff into a pair of covered wagons. You can bet they knew the meaning of hardship.

For their entire trip West, I'll bet a good horse that both of them wished that Uncle Christopher was with them. Having made the trek to California in '49 may not have made him a legend with the boys, but his duty with the army as a scout, side by side with Buffalo Bill Cody following the Civil War,

Base camps usually include a corral.

Spike camps are Spartan in nature, but allow the hunter to experience the true wilderness. (Photo courtesy of Coleman Products)

most certainly did. He had the knowledge to stay alive in the hostile setting that was the West in the 1860s and 1870s with nothing more than his saddle horse and what he could carry on him. I'd give a lot to make a month-long trip on horseback with my Uncle Chris. You can bet that I'd do a lot of listening and watching, and damn little talking, except to ask questions.

Of course, there are many combination camps in which the bulk of base camp convenience is packed back into the hunting country far from the road's end. These are perhaps the most enjoyable of all the possible camps.

Normally, base camps offer the advantages of comfort and nearly unlimited equipment lists, along with a large number of support people. You can easily get to them with trucks loaded with gear, food, and people.

Combination camps offer most of the things listed under the base camp; however, the time and cost required to get them, and you, into the backcountry is greatly inflated.

Spike camps offer the seclusion and hunting opportunities that most horseback hunters are seeking. By virtue of their location, far from the beaten path, there is very little competition from other hunters, and game is largely undisturbed, following normal patterns. In effect, the hunter is seeing the wilderness nearly as the West existed when Jim Bridger and Kit Carson explored it more than 150 years ago. On the flip side, spike camps are cold, Spartan-style survival. In the event of natural disaster or accidents, they can become dangerous. If you happen to be one of those people who cannot enjoy a picnic lunch without a solid table to eat it on, a spike camp is not for you.

It is virtually impossible for anyone to create a combination camp with one or two horses, unless they can spend several weeks doing it. The gear required to be packed demands several pack animals, in addition to saddle horses for the hunters, in order to do it in one trip. Because of this, the "average" do-it-yourself hunt must be confined to a base camp at trail's end and a few overnight forays to spike camp settings. That is how we will approach the task.

Anything from a surplus army mess tent to a self-contained RV camper, and everything in between, can become a base camp. However, there are pros and cons to everything and this topic is no different. While a tent is easy to tote nearly anywhere, it requires some expertise and much supplemental gear to erect and make livable. Since you are going to drive right to the site anyway, dragging a camp trailer, or cab-over camper to the area is not unreasonable, and when you arrive you are nearly ready to start hunting. In addition, when the wind blows and the temperature drops, the added shelter and warmth of a camper is greatly appreciated.

If you opt for the tent, one large enough for you to stand up straight inside of and containing a heated stove is a must. So also are things like bedding, cots, or at least mattress pads, a cooking stove, dishes and silverware, food,

The cab-over camper is a reasonable compromise between RVs and hard-sided camp trailers for use as a base camp; however, the top-heaviness and weight are drawbacks to be considered.

cooking pots and pans, tables, lanterns, chairs, and a myriad of other "luxury" items that make the days and nights more comfortable. All of the above are already "standard" in a camper. The only real advantage to tenting with horses is that you can haul the camp and the horse trailer with the same vehicle, something not possible with a trailer camper, but still plausible with a cab-over.

Regardless of your final decision in this matter, the stability of your vehicle choice is an often overlooked consideration. I've tried most of the various combinations listed, and here are some conclusions based on those attempts: the combination of a horse trailer and cab-over camper is both too heavy for the normal pickup truck to lug up a mountain, and too top-heavy to negotiate the uneven terrain near the camping areas at the end of a mountain road. Self-contained RVs suffer the same limitations of power and instability.

For many years, tenting was the only way I could afford to make an extended hunt. Tents work, but I can't honestly say that I enjoyed the alternate freezing or roasting, getting soaked, eating cold food when it rained or snowed, building fires with wet wood, and general discomfort that accompanied many such treks. Yes, I still put up with tents and even the rigors of not having one at all on occasion, but if you want comfort along with the enjoyment that a base camp is intended to provide, I strongly suggest a camper of some type, even if it means taking two vehicles to accommodate both the camper and the horse trailer.

In a base camp, a corral is much preferred over hobbles to restrain the urge of your horses to "join the herd." Without such an enclosure, you will constantly be chasing down errant bangtails as they attempt to follow other horses or hunters on horseback.

Such a base camp, located in drivable country, allows for the inclusion of both frozen and canned food in place of the freeze-dried and dehydrated goods which are more feasible in a pack. It also allows you to bring large tanks of fuel for cooking and heating, instead of wood.

I can only offer options and make suggestions from which

you can pick that which best suits your needs, budget, and personal wishes. I will therefore offer you a list of equipment for a tent base camp and you can alter it to fit the use of a camper based on the provisions present in whatever type of rig you may have. The list will narrow greatly when you decide to spend a night or two at a spike camp.

Outfitters have a decided advantage when it comes to setting up camps. No matter if it is a base camp, spike camp, or combination, they may do all the work of packing in, constructing, and provisioning prior to the hunting season. By the time you arrive as a client, the hard work has all been done. As a do-it-yourself hunter, all of this work remains ahead of you as you leave home. If at all possible, a pre-hunt trip to the area will allow you to at least pick out several suitable sites and know where you are going. I say pick several for the simple reason that what is a secluded and deserted meadow or clearing in September can become a miniature city in October during big game hunting season. You may very well find your preselected site taken when you arrive.

LIST OF BASE CAMP NEEDS

Axe/saw
Batteries
Books/magazines
Chairs
Clothing
Cooking stove/fuel
Cooking utensils
Coolers
Cots/pads
Dishes
Dish-washing items
Drinking water
Eating utensils
First-aid kit
Flashlight
Food
Heating stove/pipe

Horse feed
Ice
Insect netting
Insect repellent
Lantern
Matches
Nails/wire
Personal bathing items
Porta-potty/latrine
Ropes
Shovel
Sleeping bags
Storage containers
Table
Tarps
Tent pegs/poles
Wall tent

A compass is a must in backcountry. (Photo courtesy of Michaels of Oregon)

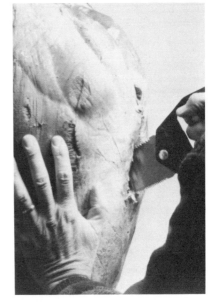

A belt saw can do multiple tasks, and is therefore worth the space it takes up when you pack. (Photo courtesy of Michaels of Oregon)

When packing in, items must do double duty. (Photo courtesy of Coleman Products)

Lanterns are useful in base camp. (Photo courtesy of Coleman Products)

Compact heaters and stoves may be worth the extra weight in cold weather. (Photo courtesy of Coleman Products)

When it comes to picking a campsite, it matters very little if you are tenting or using a camper. Basic needs remain, as do considerations of safety. The spot should be reasonably level and well drained, supply a source of water for the horses to drink from, and not be exposed to floods or unbroken winds. If there is a public campground on National Forest Land near your hunting area, this is an excellent place to consider for a base.

In bear country, common sense and federal law require that you make provisions for deterring the wandering bruins from ravaging your food supplies, garbage, and any game taken. Those laws require that game be hung at specified distances from camp and off the ground. Be sure to check with forest rangers or forest management offices before making your plans so that you will have the required material to conform with any laws in effect in your hunting area. It should be obvious that storing food in a sleeping tent is asking for trouble in bear territory. The same is true of horse feed, especially any grains mixed with molasses. These should all be suspended at least ten feet off the ground and away from the tree trunk where they will be out of harm's way.

A final consideration when planning menus and other garbage-producing equipment lists is that everything that you haul in must be hauled out, unless it is burnable. In that regard, boxes and bags as packaging are superior in that you need not haul them around empty.

Regardless of how extensive your camping experience, you will come to realize that something new is learned on every outing. By virtue of that, feel free to substitute, alter, or otherwise change my suggestions to fit your own needs.

Chapter 7

Packing with Horses

The topic of horse packing could form the basis for a book in itself if we were to delve into it with a true passion. Because of this, and because it will not be a book in itself, suffice it to say that the information contained here will not be the only suitable methods that may be used, nor even always the best. It will rather be a smattering of things that work and will be feasible for the average hunter who is taking his own horses hunting, or who has booked a guided hunt and needs some basic information for the purpose of preparing his list of gear to take along.

If you are going on a commercial horseback hunt and the initial move from civilization will be aboard a horse and not by motor vehicle, there will be a limit in terms of weight and bulk which the pack animals can carry. Each outfit will have its own specifications of which you should be advised early on. Unless you are willing to pay through the nose for a personal safari, you can logically expect that weight limit to fall between 70 and 150 pounds. For the do-it-yourselfer, this higher figure is a good upper limit to shoot for in terms of a load for one horse to carry packed on its back. Of course, there are exceptions to this rule. A saddle horse routinely carries between 200 and 300 pounds when you add tack to rider, plus hunting equipment. The main difference here is that in cases of extremely difficult terrain, poor footing, and

other factors, the rider can dismount and let the horse function in nearly a natural state. Pack animals, on the other
hand, must bear their load all day, over every foot of the
trail.

For this reason alone, pack animals should not be over-
loaded. In addition to that, however, on the way back out,
there may be additional weight in the form of meat and
antlers to be borne by the same animals. It is therefore
imperative that they not be loaded to maximum capacity
at the onset.

The most burdensome load a pack animal will carry is
the game taken from the kill site to the camp or vehicles.
When the downed species is an elk or moose, this load may
approach 400 pounds for those periods. So once again, we
see the benefits of preplanning.

While there are many fortunate folks who own or have
access to a string of horses which can be pressed into service
for a pack-in hunt, most horse owners in the world have only
one or two horses which must bear the brunt of the expe-
dition. It is these conditions at which this material will
be aimed in order to make this type of hunt feasible.

Let's assume that we have two saddle horses and a spare
animal to pack on, and two hunters with their gear to get
into the mountains. Yes, I hear all of you who only have one
horse moaning, but don't toss this in the corner yet. I'll
cover that shoestring operation in a few pages more. Oh yes,
it can be done with one!

With the pack animal there are numerous saddle arrange-
ments available that are tried and true, but in reality, they all
boil down to a basic design altered in some way. For this
reason, we will discuss two: the crossbuck pack saddle,
whether it involves boxes, lashed gear, or baskets, and the
pannier made to fit over a standard riding saddle. With either
one of these two rigs, we can handle the job. If you use some
other names which apply to your equipment, changing the
wording as you read is easier than trying to explain every
variation that may exist in the world of horseback hunters.

Crossbuck pack saddles allow you to lash on loads of gear

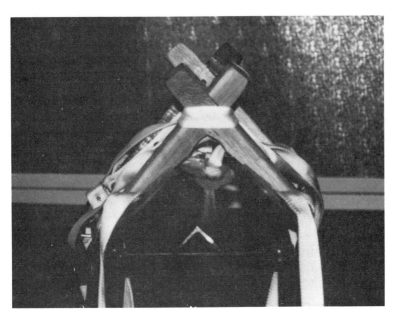

Crossbuck pack saddles offer secure lashing points.

Panniers are easy and cheap for the once-a-year hunter, and offer a lot of support for loads.

or meat with a reasonable amount of security and a minimum of wasted weight. Saddle panniers will do the job and are probably more common for the do-it-yourself addict for several reasons: they look easier to use, they are cheaper to buy, and it is easier to borrow a riding saddle than a pack saddle. In both cases, there are certain basic rules that apply.

Regardless of the base you choose to put on the animal's back, the load must be even. This is rule one for any packing operation. In other words, if there is seventy pounds on the right side, there must be pretty close to seventy pounds on the left. The next bit of advice should become a rule if it isn't already: The load ought to build up and in, not up and out. If the load gets extremely wide, you will soon find that the trail is too narrow for the pack to slip through and it will end up being ripped from the horse. By the same token, if the pile looks like an inverted pyramid, it will soon succumb to the force that Newton termed "gravity," and topple to the surface of the terra firma. Worse, it will probably slide part way and the bucking that will ensue will scatter "junk" that used to be expensive—and needed—gear all over the mountainside. Last, the exterior of the sides of any pack should contain the hard, unbreakable, unyielding items while the interior, closest to the horse, should be made up of the soft, and fragile items.

In regard to lashing the loads in place, there are as many "accepted" and "only" ways to do so as there are brands or makes of vehicles on the highway. Without offending anyone, it really doesn't matter which rope, lashing, knot, or combination of loops and crossovers you employ. What does matter is this: all of the knots must be secure while remaining easy to untie. All of the lashings must support and secure the load that they are meant to attach to the mobile platform carrying them. The surest way to firmly establish that combination of ingredients is to practice until you find something that you can repeatedly master, and that works for you. If the ropes support the bottom, sides, and ends of the pack with the weight being borne from the top and center of the saddle, it will work.

Any items which are too long or too bulky to fit into the packs should be lashed down lengthwise on the top of the load, and then bound over with a tarp or other strong covering. Out of pure economy of space, all normally empty containers should be filled with smaller articles to make use of that otherwise unused space inside the packs. For instance, if you are taking a coffeepot or Dutch oven, fill the interior with packages of seasoning, spices, silverware, or food. In this manner, you will fill the packs to true capacity without wasting any room that is so scarce to begin with.

While you cannot take everything that you might dream up, you will find that a single pack animal can carry enough equipment to make a comfortable camp for two hunters with very little hardship to them or the draft animal. Trying to make the trip with only the saddle horse will not be the same, but as I said, it can be done.

The trick to getting along on one horse to carry both you and your gear is relatively simple: you must learn to make do with as little equipment as is humanly possible. Here are some thoughts on what that means. You can no doubt expand the possibilities using your own imagination once you get into the swing of things. Instead of a cooking kit, plan to get by on improvised materials. A single canteen cup which fits right over the canteen you take to carry your water in will serve to boil water to rehydrate packages of food. When that is done, you can make coffee or tea in the cup with the extra hot water left over after making the meal in the foil pouch as the instructions call for. This should clue you in on the use of freeze-dried, or dehydrated, food in place of fresh or canned victuals.

Forget about a tent. You can get by on a lean-to made from pine boughs, a folded polyethylene sheet, or a space blanket. You can sleep in relative comfort in insulated coveralls and a space blanket instead of a sleeping bag. Forget gallons of pure water and rely on boiling and purification tablets to provide it. The list goes on, but the point should be made by now: make do on as little as possible.

I have hunted in this manner and it is by no means impossible or grossly uncomfortable. On the other hand, it is not something that is recommended for anyone who has not lived off the land, had a practical survival course, or is in any way a stranger to the wilderness. To try something like this as a first adventure in the wild is asking for tragedy. Like anything, work into it gradually, and if you are a novice, be satisfied to operate out of a base camp on your first hunt on horseback.

This is all well and good you say, but how do you get the game out with only one horse and no packs? Well, first of all, you walk out leading the horse. This is still infinitely easier than doing the same with a backpack frame. Secondly, you don't need a pack saddle or panniers to pack out a gutted animal. Smaller game like mule deer can be tied onto the saddle with rope and be taken out whole. Larger animals like elk and moose must be handled in pieces. With a compact block and tackle, you can get the animal out in two trips if you don't want the head.

Begin by cutting the gutted carcass in two at the saddle behind the ribs. You now have a set of hind quarters and a set of front quarters with the rib cage attached. You have the choice of removing the loins and rib meat, or hauling it out intact. The decision is largely a matter of personal taste, distance, and terrain to be covered. Next, cut the legs at the knee joints and discard the lower portion. Then, cut the head and neck off at the junction with the chest and front shoulders. The meat on the neck can be stripped off and carried in the saddlebags, like the loin.

Using the hatchet, cut through the bone and muscle from the inside until you reach the inner surface of the hide. Make an incision with your knife that will allow you to slip the center of the splayed half over the saddle horn of your riding saddle. By raising the section into a tree with the block and tackle, you can place it on the horse and tie it in place. The remaining leg should be stuck through the stirrup on each side of the saddle and also tied in place.

Now we come to an area that many of you are not going to believe until you try it. Prove me wrong if you like, but

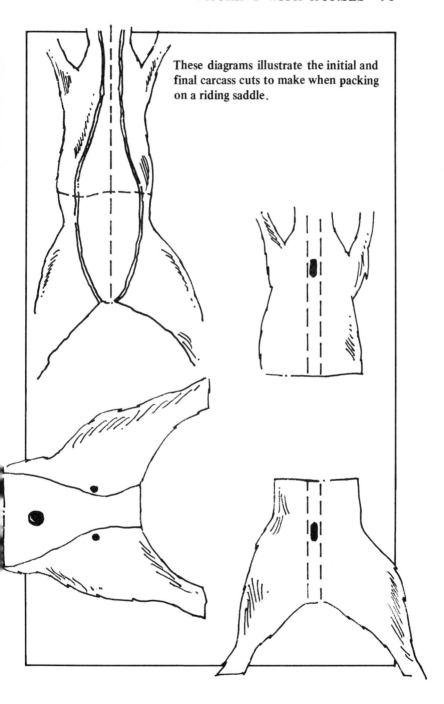

These diagrams illustrate the initial and final carcass cuts to make when packing on a riding saddle.

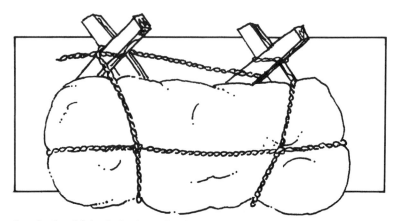

Loads should be lashed to the horse to give support to the sides and bottoms of your packs.

if I've heard it once, I've heard it a hundred times: "My horses all are very well-broke, gentle, riding horses that will carry anybody."

The therefore that follows that infamous utterance is, "so, they will pack!" The last two times that I heard that statement made, punctuated by a fist impacting on an open palm, we had a magnificent learning experience. Nothing that I would call fun was associated with it, however.

The first time it entailed packing equipment for a few nights in the Wyoming wilderness where no motorized vehicles are permitted. The saddle horse packed the gear in okay. It was on the way out when a lashing let loose and the pack began swinging that the ol' girl decided to prove us wrong. After spewing equipment over an eighty-acre meadow twice, down a sheer drop into a canyon once, and cutting her pastern to the bone, followed by rolling down the upper shale slide of the canyon to catch herself within inches of the rim, her packing days were over. This, of course, meant that we had to make an extra trip to carry out the gear we could find and recover once we had limped her the ten miles to the base camp. That little escapade took one day out of a week's hunt, not to mention the loss of a horse for the duration of the season.

The next time this phenomenon reared up on a hunt was while packing a load of elk meat and hide out. The normally gentle saddle horse took one look at the carcass, sniffed the scent filling the air around the kill and with wild eyes, flaring nostrils, and laid-back ears refused to get near the quartered wapiti. We finally coaxed the intended pack animal close enough to load a front shoulder and the hide, and we even got it lashed in place. All of this was accomplished with the horse blindfolded using a bandanna. Thankfully, we were using two pack horses and two lead mounts that day, for the second the blinders came off, the skittish horse rolled its head to the load on its back, did a slapstick comedian's double take and lit out for the low country in high gear. Had the other pack animal been tied to the first, it would have been even worse. As it was, the horse, load of meat, and the pack saddle all ended up in a rib-heaving, mass of quivering exhaustion at a ranch several miles from our embarkation point.

That was the last time I believed the false assumption that led us into that fiasco. If an animal has never packed, there is no reason to assume that it will do so. Try to find out for sure, prior to making a hunt, if the animal can handle the situations you'll be expecting of it.

What happens if you own a horse that will learn to pack equipment, but still goes crazy in the presence of a dead animal? Sometimes you live with the fact, sometimes you trade horses. There are two things that may work. They are not guaranteed, but worth a try if you really don't want to get rid of the horse or have it pull only half its weight. The first thing you can try is to make the horse live with the hide of the animal you intend to pack on it. Hang the offending hide in the pasture, corral, or stall for the year between hunting seasons. By the end of that time, you should be able to lead the horse to the hide, lay it on the animal's back, and in general, have it treated like a saddle blanket without the fear reaction occurring.

If that doesn't do the trick, there is a last resort that I've seen work, although I can't give you a completely scientific explanation for why or how. With the horse secured to a completely immovable object using an unbreakable lead, smear the animal's muzzle with the fresh blood of the game he so fears. If that fails, forget it. You must face the fact that it is a hopeless case.

By the way, oh ye of little faith, I know that getting fresh blood from a game animal is illegal except during a season for which you have a license to hunt the species. But, if you will take the time to plan, you can legally acquire the serum. Contact your local game warden and explain your need for a hide, or the hemoglobin. These public servants have access to every bit of road kill, poached animal, or confiscated portions around. If you ask, you may well find a small bottle of the needed material deposited into your hand by a smiling conservation officer one bright day, or dark night. It is also a possibility that your hunting friends will make an effort to provide you with a fresh hide from a legal kill if you check right before and after season.

Regardless of all else, check the situation out thoroughly before you make up your mind that your hunting horse will pack anything.

LIST OF GEAR FOR A SINGLE-HORSE, OVERNIGHT HUNT

Ammo	Gloves
Belt saw	Grain
Block and tackle	Hat
Boots	Hatchet
Canteen	Hobbles
Canteen cup	Instant beverages
Coat	Insulated coveralls
Compass/maps	Knife
Emergency clothing	Lariat
Face mask	Purification tablets
First-aid kit	Rain gear
Flashlight	Rifle
Freeze-dried food	Saddle

Saddlebags
Scabbard
Soap/towel
Space blankets (two)

Spoon
Sunglasses
Toilet paper
Waterproof matches

Feel free to modify or adjust this list to fit your own needs. If, for instance, you cannot picture a night without a sleeping bag, add it in and subtract the coveralls. Emergency clothes are not something to compromise on, however. If you get drenched and the temperature goes below zero, they will save your life.

Chapter 8
Rifles & Ammo

We have finally arrived at that portion in this collection of thoughts, suggestions, and beliefs that all of you old hands have been waiting for. The chance to find out if I am a student of Elmer Keith and use a 20mm antitank gun whenever possible, or a devotee of Jack O'Conner and the omniscient .270 which, in his opinion, could take anything created of flesh and bone.

As much as I respect both these giants of the industry, I guess I fall somewhere between them in terms of firearm philosophy.

If I personally had to own only one centerfire rifle, I would be hard-pressed to choose between my two all-time favorites. Elmer would shudder that I might opt for something as small as the .300 Winchester Magnum, but that is as large as my caliber choices extend. Jack could well question my lack of benevolence in choosing the .243 Winchester over his beloved .270, but in my heart, that is the only caliber that would have a chance to overthrow the .300.

Regardless of which of my two considerations were to win this mystical conflict, there are several things that would not change in the outfitting of the weapon for a horseback hunt. Any rifle that I own for the purpose of expending cartridges would have a sling. Not only for the sake of making it easier to tote around on my shoulder—a task it performs well and

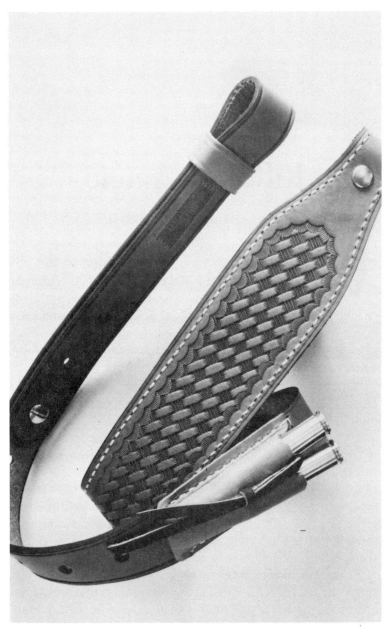

A sling is a wise investment, even on a horseback hunt. (Photo courtesy of Michaels of Oregon)

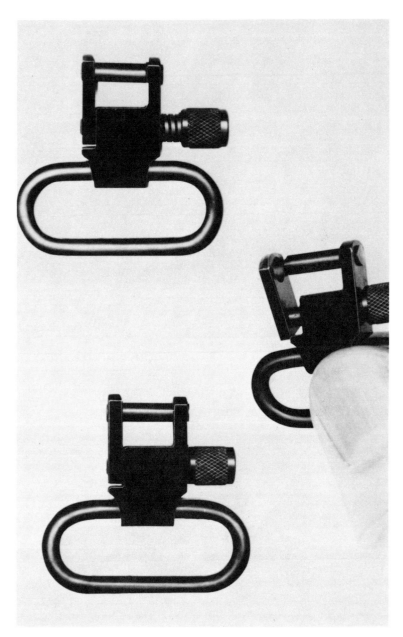

Examples of quick detachable swivels for sling use. (Photo courtesy of Michaels of Oregon)

Gun Chaps (trademark of Kane Products) can save an expensive stock from abuse.

Iron sights, scopes, and mounts are all a matter of personal choice.

that should not be overlooked—but as an aid in sighting when a sandbag rest is not handy. That condition pops up quite frequently on a hunt, by the way.

Attached to that leather sling would be a set of quick-detachable swivels. Each swivel would be carefully lubricated with WD-40 or other silicone to eliminate any squeaks as it rocks on the studs embedded in the rifle stock.

On the receiver of my rifle, you will find pivot mounts and rings containing a 3x9 variable scope with a 4-plex style of reticule. Now, there are probably already screams mimicking a gut-shot hyena coming from those dyed-in-the-wool proponents of rigid scope mounts on anything larger than a BB gun, but they won't change my mind. Over the past twenty years, I have never used a mount that didn't swing over to allow me to use the open sights if and when the scope was broken, fogged, or full of rain, snow, or dirt. Not once in that time have those pivot mounts been out of place when I needed them, nor has any zero changed because of them. If you don't like them, you don't need to use them! For me, see-through mounts set the scope too high and sighting becomes unnatural.

Now there is nothing special about a 3x9 scope, and if you don't care for variable-power glass, by all means stick with something you do like. That is the essence of my feeling about guns, ammunition, and shooting in general. If it feels good and you get acceptable results, forget the opinion of the so-called experts and have at it. A scope can't make you an expert rifleman if you are normally so inept that you can't hit the broad side of a barn from the inside. But with practiced marksmanship, a scope can let you place your shots in a vital area that might otherwise be obscured by brush or grass. If you can see which part of the animal is exposed, and are thus able to hit a vital spot rather than "some" part of that quarry, you stand a better chance of taking the trophy home. In other words, having a scope may mean that you can take a shot which you would have to pass up with open sights.

With those pivot mounts, of course, my rifles have good

iron sights. The front sight is a ramp carrying a fine bead of ivory, silver, or gold. The rear sight is a fully adjustable, flat-topped, U-notched sight with a white diamond, or triangle, pointing the way to the base of the U.

Complementing the scope and mounts would be a scope cover that is instantly removable. Such covers are desirable for the simple reason that I don't like having to clean snow, rain, or dirt off the lenses.

A bolt-action rifle is my first hunting choice, not because I have anything against pumps, lever-actions, or semiautomatics, but because of the bolt-action's versatility, accuracy, and sure function. I own and use all of the other action types, but even the most dedicated afficionado of these various actions will have to admit that they are more fussy about the ammo they digest when compared to bolt-actions. A bolt-action magazine and chamber will take a variety of bullet designs. This certainly cannot be said for the tubular magazines often found on lever- and certain pump-action guns which demand flat-nosed bullets to prevent detonation in the magazine during recoil.

While we are on bullet design, let's make still another valiant effort to put to rest an old adage that simply doesn't hold up under actual testing. When I was just a pup, nearly every gun writer in the country agreed that a Spitzer-style bullet was too fast and too pointed to be of any use in brush country. By that same theory, flat-nosed, or even round, tips on big, heavy, slow-moving bullets were the brush-bucking kings. In reality, test after test has proven that not only do the big, slow monsters not buck twigs any better than a spire point, but in lots of instances they do a *worse* job. Don't be misled by rumors and stories. Check it out yourself and then decide.

In addition to the variety of bullet designs it will accept, the bolt-action will close on slightly oversized cartridges and still fire. Bolts stand higher pressures and continue to function under adverse conditions where less sturdy actions fail. And while there are exceptions, the average bolt-action will be more accurate than the average rifle featuring any other

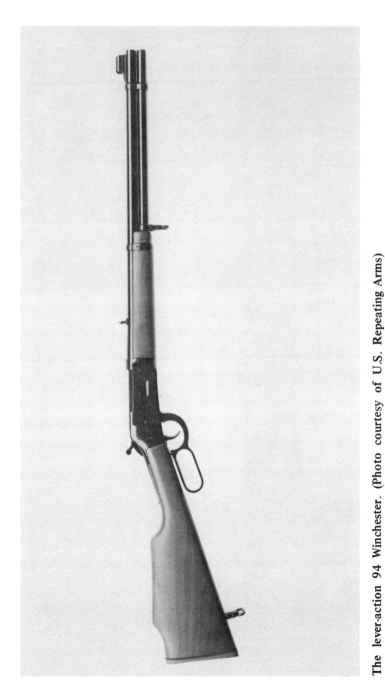

The lever-action 94 Winchester. (Photo courtesy of U.S. Repeating Arms)

The slide-action (pump) Remington 760.

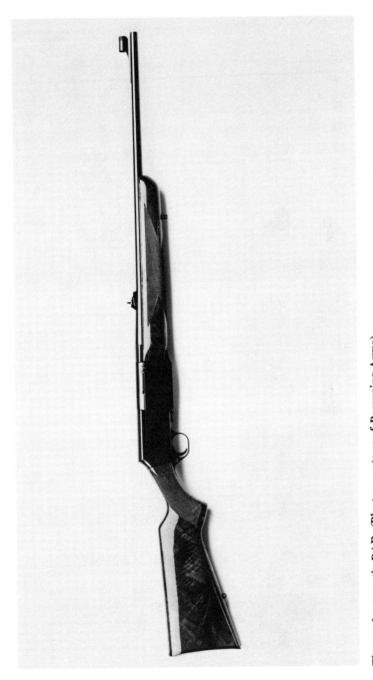

The semiautomatic BAR. (Photo courtesy of Browning Arms)

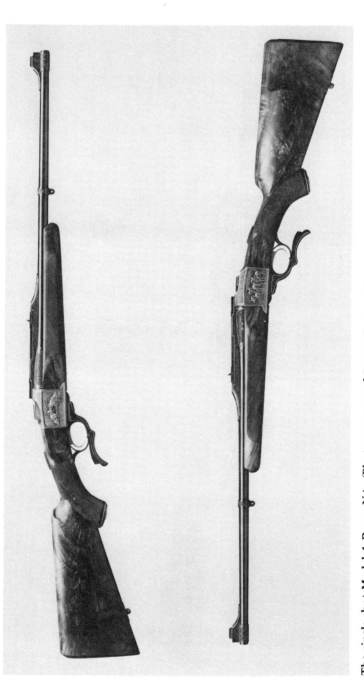

The single-shot Model 1 Ruger NA. (Photo courtesy of Sturm, Ruger & Company)

RUGER M-77RL *ULTRA LIGHT* 6 POUNDS - 20˝ BARREL

The bolt-action Model 77 Ruger. (Photo courtesy of Sturm, Ruger & Company)

type of action.

In terms of what you ought to use to hunt with, none of my action, scope, mount, or caliber choices are very important. What is important are three basic considerations:

Can the caliber do the job you will ask it to perform?

Are you totally familiar and confident with the firearm?

Can you hit what you aim at using the weapon and ammunition of your choice?

Taking those considerations in order, let's assume that what some people say is true: "The .243 is a marginal deer cartridge at best and has no value on an elk hunt." Well, I don't recommend a .243 for elk for the simple reason that it won't consistently punch a hole through a shoulder blade, which may be the only shot you'll get. But I do allow my sons to hunt elk with the little gem. I've seen many elk killed with one .243 bullet of 100 grains through the lungs, and we have never lost an elk so shot. The reason that I let the boys use a .243 on elk is threefold. First, they hit exactly where they aim. This means only the heart/lung area—not the shoulder, not head shots, and no attempts at oblique-angled or long shots.

While on that topic, when was the last time you went to a range and actually fired for effect? I recall that when I was in college, I thought that after ten years of shooting, I was good! It took only a few visits to the local rifle club to prove how wrong that assumption was. After another four years of shooting everything from .22s in the winter to shotguns and high-powers in the summer, I managed to win the club trophy for highest yearly score with the high-powered rifle. Some years later, I took several first-place awards in police combat pistol competition, and shot consistent 23-24-25s on the trap range. Still, I miss from time to time and the practice never ends. If you think you're good, go shoot a competition match.

The second thing that made me decide to let the boys hunt elk with the .243 was that they couldn't handle the recoil of a .300 Winchester Magnum, nor even a .30-06. They couldn't shoot them well enough to be sure of a clean kill.

What good do .30-caliber holes in the air around an animal do?

Last, they have confidence in their weapons, and know exactly what they can and can't do under all conditions. Sounds familiar, doesn't it? Even at that, I was at first leery about the practice, given all the negative information I had heard in regard to light bullets and elk. It took only one hunt and one shot to change my mind. My eldest son, Jamie, took his .243 on his first elk hunt and with one shot at 200 yards dropped a 600-pound dry cow with a well-placed lung shot.

It isn't only a matter of knowing the range and trajectory of the cartridge/rifle combination that you have chosen. I recall vividly how switching from my custom-built .300 Winchester Magnum to a factory Model 70 Winchester in the same caliber cost me an elk one year. It had nothing to do with accuracy levels, ammunition specifications, or the ability to hit with the rifle. It was a simple matter of having a safety that pushed ahead instead of flipping down with one stroke of my thumb. By the time the message got through to my brain and back to my thumb, the elk was gone in the black timber. Little things mean a lot!

The point of all this is easy to form into a synopsis—if you are comfortable using a pump, don't go out and buy a bolt-action just because someone tells you it is slightly more accurate, somewhat stronger, or less apt to malfunction. Stick with what you are confident in using. If you've shot a lever-action for years, don't switch to a semiauto just to change cartridges. Get something in a lever that handles a comparable load.

Few people will suggest, least of all me, that a .30-30 is the ultimate elk load. As a matter of fact, in my opinion it isn't worth spit for anything over 150 yards. Yet, if you had all the game ever taken with this round, you could feed the world for several days. In any case, most of these kills were out of necessity or cartridge availability and there is no need to limit yourself. That same lever-action can be found chambering some damn fine long-range, flat-trajectory shells. Among the better big-game-caliber choices, taking various manufacturers into account, are: .264, .270, .280, .284, .307, .308, .338, .356, and .375.

Stick with what you know and trust in terms of actions. Don't overgun yourself to the point of inaccuracy but do have something which is capable of doing the job. In other words, make the weapon and cartridge fit the need and your own limitations. The key to successful hunting is to plan, consider options, and then compromise.

There is nothing magical about the .300 or 7mm Magnum, nor any other caliber. The only reason for using any souped-up cartridge is to add range and impact that will result in a clean kill. I have actually seen a bull elk take a hit in the forehead with a .30-06 and live through the experience. This wasn't because the caliber isn't an elk slayer. It is! It was a combination of extended range and poor angle of impact. The bullet simply slid under the skin and over the heavy skull plate. A .338 may not have done any better in the same situation. Range and shot placement then become the prime factors in taking game.

With these considerations in mind, we come back to that 4-plex scope reticule that was mentioned earlier. With that rig, you can judge distance quite reliably by knowing two factors: how much space in inches there is between the wider portions of the crosshair at the range you have zeroed for, and the average size of the animal hunted. By seeing how much of that space the animal fills, you can tell how far away it is. For instance, if an elk averages thirty inches in height from chest to shoulder line, and the scope's crosshair separation is six inches at 100 yards, then at 400 yards you are looking at twenty-four inches and he isn't going to fit inside that opening. At 500 yards, however, you see thirty inches, and he will exactly fit inside the brackets. If all that is too complicated for you, buy a scope that has a range finder built in.

The next thing is shot placement, and that brings up the story of the 1,000-yard shot in the eye. That tale is definitely BS! At 1,000 yards, a .30-06 is dropping too fast and unpredictably for anyone to hit consistently.

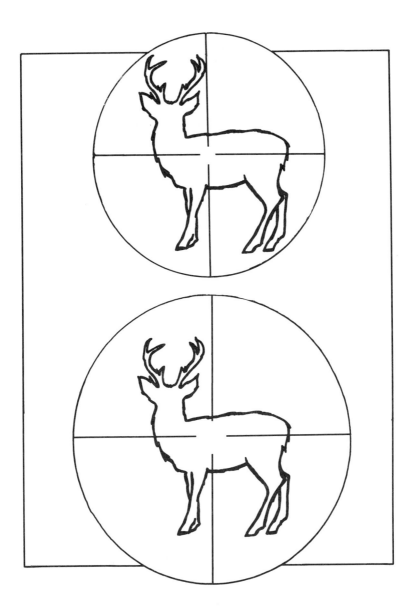

Range determination using six-inch scope reticle on an eighteen-inch deer body. Top figure shows the deer at 100 yards, with one-third of the body covered. Bottom figure shows the deer at 200 yards, with two-thirds of the body covered, and . . .

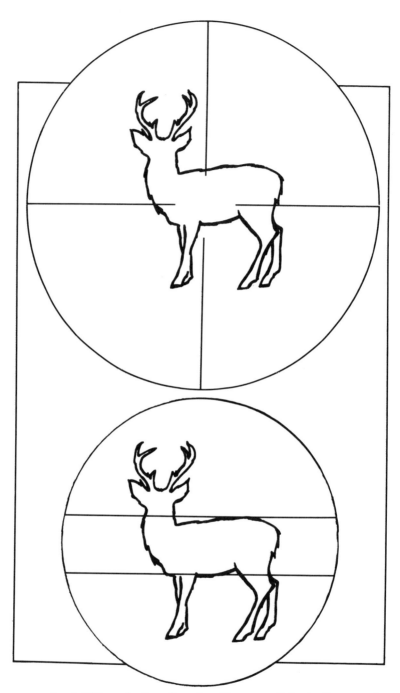

... again at 300 yards (top figure), with none of the body covered. Bottom figure illustrates range determination using range finder feature. Some scopes allow you to bracket the target and read the range directly.

You show me anyone who can shoot well enough to actually aim at the eye on the animal and hit it from 1,000 yards, and I'll buy him a drink!

But what about those fluke hits at 1,000 yards? They do happen; I've seen it. Well, luck can't end with just the hit, because I have personally shot silhouettes at 1,000 yards using a .30-06 loaded with 180-grain bullets and factory powder charges, only to have that steel target sit on its perch as if untouched, despite the resounding clang of the bullet connecting. There is so little energy left in the bullet at that range that penetration is nearly nonexistent.

Regardless of luck, tall tales, or just plain greed, 500 yards is really pushing it under most conditions. Learn to limit yourself to your own effective range and that of your rifle and load. If you sight in at 225 yards, you can hold "right on" anything within reasonable range and hit it.

If you don't own a rifle and intend to go out and buy one, I suggest that you choose from the following list of chamberings, and that you actually fire the type of weapon that you think you want prior to plunking down hard cash for it.

LIST OF BIG GAME CARTRIDGES

.243 Winchester	6mm Remington
.25-06 Remington	.264 Winchester Magnum
.270 Winchester	7mm Mauser (7x57)
7mm-08 Remington	.280 Remington
7mm Remington Magnum	.307 Winchester
.308 Winchester	.30-06 Springfield
.35 Remington	.300 H&H Magnum
.300 Winchester Magnum	8mm Remington Magnum
.338 Winchester Magnum	.350 Remington Magnum
.356 Winchester	.375 Winchester

Or, you may wish to pick from any of the Weatherby versions of the above list.

While we are mentioning Roy Weatherby's fine weapons, it is important to make a seldom-discussed point. If you are

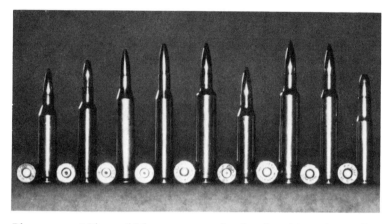

Big-game cartridges which are commonly chambered in today's rifles. Proper application depends on the shooter's ability. From left to right, the cartridges are: .243, 6mm, 25-06, .270, .270 Weatherby, 7mm-08, 7mm Weatherby Magnum, .280, 30-30.

going to have an apoplexy when a scratch appears on a thousand-dollar stock, don't buy such a fine weapon for hunting. Save it to hang on the wall, or get a protective cover for it, such as the Kane Gun Chaps. After all, what is another thirty dollars or so to maintain an investment of such magnitude? Carrying a rifle in an unhooded scabbard in timber can make it look like someone beat it with a chain before the week ends.

You hear a lot of discussion about what makes for a perfect "mountain rifle." If you lug your typical heavyweight rifle up and down a few slopes, you'll soon see why such a weapon developed. Requirements for a mountain rifle fall into two areas. First and foremost is weight (and balance), followed by chambering.

There are numerous ways to lighten a rifle, not the least of which is to replace the stock with one made of fiberglass. However, you need not be too concerned about the rifle's weight on a horseback hunt, so remember that as the weight of the rifle decreases, so does your ability to hold a steady sight picture. Before you head down to the local sports store to buy an ultra-light, consider whether or not you are going to rob Peter to pay Paul.

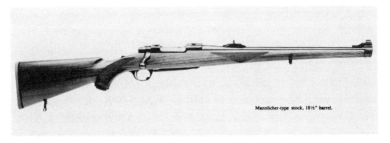

An eighteen-inch barrel is easier to handle in comparison to a twenty-four-inch tube, without adversely affecting range or power. (Photo courtesy of Sturm, Ruger & Company)

A standard wooden stock adds heft for steady sighting. (Photo courtesy of U.S. Repeating Arms)

Another area of controversy that never ends is the "best" barrel length. To hear some tell it, we are still burning black powder, and every inch of tube counts for increased velocity. In reality, there isn't five cents' worth of difference between a twenty-six-inch and an eighteen-inch barrel, except weight and balance. Don't saddle yourself with something unwieldy to satisfy an antique idea.

You'll notice that I have not addressed the topic of hunting with a handgun or single-shot rifle. The reason is quite simple. If you are good enough to hunt with those weapons, you already know everything that I can tell you about the topic, or at least think you do!

To recap my recommendations for a horseback-hunting arm, pick a rifle with an action that you are comfortable using. The caliber should be large enough to do the job you intend for it to accomplish, without going beyond your capacity to handle it. Equip your choice with a sling, and the type of sights you prefer, be it a scope, or iron sights. Once you have that combination complete, sight in at 225 yards, then practice, practice, practice! When you know exactly what you and the rifle are capable of doing together, learn to judge distance and don't take shots beyond that limit which you have established for yourself.

If there is one thing that a rifleman who chooses to use a caliber in the .300 Winchester Magnum category hates to hear, it is the ridiculous statement made by people who think power can compensate for lack of skill. It goes something like this: "If I can hit it anywhere, it's dead." That is pure garbage in its unadulterated form. To gut-shoot a fine trophy in hopes that it will die on the spot instead of crawling off into the timber to spend days suffering for no useful purpose is both ignorant and thoughtless. The man who can't hit an animal in the kill zone with reasonable certainty has no business shooting at it, regardless of what he might be toting around for armament.

Chapter 9

Tack & Equipment

We've hinted at it, skimmed over it, even tackled it directly in one or two spots. Now we get to the nitty-gritty of what you should and shouldn't put atop a hunting horse.

I can't think of a better place to start than with the saddle. Whether hunting alone or on a guided trip, you may wish to have your own saddle along. If at all possible, practice with the actual saddle you'll be using, prior to the hunt. Do not make the mistake of waiting until the day before the planned departure date to buy that beautiful, tooled, handcrafted saddle that you've been drooling over for years. Why not? Because the noise of all that new leather working in will not only drive you crazy, it will spook everything worth hunting within miles. I honestly don't know of anything to replace hard riding when it comes to taking the squeak out of new leather. You simply have to ride it prior to the hunt to make it quiet enough to be of use rather than a detriment. In addition, how do you know if the rig is comfortable if you don't ride it?

If you are now asking which saddle to buy, you get us back into the equipment battlefield. I will make a few generalizations, but bear in mind that you will be spending the better parts of many days in the rig that you choose, and comfort, as you see it or feel it, is foremost. In addition, the hunting saddle serves several purposes which should be taken into account if you are buying one for that activity only.

The latigo has to hold one hell of a bunch of weight on a hunting saddle. First, it will retain your saddlebags and any "extras" like your coat or your insulated coveralls. While the saddle shop may not care much for the practice, I'd strain that set of leather straps to the utmost in the shop before I put a cent out for a new horse seat. If you can get away with it, snapping the latigo several times with a grip on the ends and using all the slack for leverage will show you most flaws in the leather.

Contrary to what I've read in several highly respected articles and books dealing with horseback hunts, I do not personally know of any knowledgeable rider who will use the latigo as an anchor point for a rifle scabbard. This task is usually, and ought to always be, relegated to such heavy-duty points as the saddlebow, D-rings, or stirrup leathers. Not to do so is asking for a lost rifle and a torn-up saddle. In relation to that function, finding you can't bend your knee around a rifle in a scabbard under the stirrup leather is an all-too-common experience on the first day of a hunt. I cannot do it with anything having more bulk than a standard saddle carbine.

As you can see in the photographs, it is possible to hang a scabbard from the pommel and attach the bottom strap to the stirrup leather or cinch, and not have to contend with a bulge under your leg at all. In choosing to use this arrangement, there are factors to consider that you may not think of until it is too late. One of these is that the bottom strap has to be very tight to prevent the lower portion of the boot from swinging excessively and smacking the horse on each step. The second is that, while being mounted where you can keep an eye on it, it is also in an excellent position to snag up on saplings and low-hanging limbs as you ride in timber. If you try to hang the scabbard upright on the rear of the saddle, you must clear the protruding buttstock in order to mount or dismount. By pointing the muzzle forward in a

Forward-mounted scabbard is not best when you are riding through trees, but if used, should be secured to the pommel, and the rigging or stirrup leather, not the saddle latigo.

A rearward-mounted scabbard is most likely to lose its cargo if it is not hooded or equipped with a retaining strap. Note the attachment to the D-ring and cinch leather. Scabbards on the horse's left are easier to reach from the ground.

The latigo should be strong, and long enough to function as it was intended. (Photo courtesy of Michaels of Oregon)

nearly horizontal position, you run the risk that a bush or tree limb will snag the rifle and pull it from the boot as you ride. It is not unusual to lose a rifle in this manner, especially if you have a sling protruding from the scabbard and no retaining strap or hood.

Using a hooded scabbard always sounds like the thing to do, at least until you need the rifle in a hurry. When that occurs, the single strap becomes infinitely more desirable to a lot of folks, and I've seen many a scabbard disappear after the first day of use.

Another thing about scabbards that we touched on earlier is that they should fit the rifle you intend to carry in them. Not only does this mean that the boot should be large enough to accommodate the weapon, but also that it should not be so oversized that the rifle has room to bang around inside it.

As much as I like a hooded front sight on a rifle, they do not get along particularly well with tight-fitting scabbards.

If the sight hood does not pull off and lie in the bottom of the rifle boot when you draw it out, it will hang up and hold the rifle in the sheath when you need it most. If the scabbard is lined, you can bet the hood will tear that material to shreds in short order.

There is one consideration of safety that seems self-evident, yet goes unheeded year after year in terms of carrying a weapon on a horse. Not only can the gun fall several feet during an accident, but all the jockeying in and out during the course of a normal day's hunt can slip a safety catch, or pull a trigger. If you note the general position of the rifle muzzle in the scabbard, you will see that an accidental discharge will most likely eliminate your ride if it occurs. The chamber should be empty while the rifle is being carried. I don't know anyone who has accidentally shot the horse he was mounted on, but I have heard of this happening from men I believe without question, and it is certainly enough of a possibility to avoid taking the chance. To prove the point a bit further, let me relate another tale that is fully recorded in fact.

It was a beautiful April day on the plains of Kansas when a young and brash graduate of West Point decided to detach himself from duty long enough to do a bit of hunting and sight-seeing. Miles from his command, the officer came upon a buffalo and gave chase mounted on his thoroughbred horse. Getting up next to the beast with his weapon cocked and ready to dispatch it, the tables turned as the buffalo lunged toward the horse and rider. In the split second of instinctive avoidance, the weapon discharged and the bullet shattered the horse's brain at a full gallop, leaving the shaken man to walk home many miles in hostile territory.

While brevet General George Armstrong Custer seldom, if ever, made note of the fact that he shot his own horse from the saddle, the incident did not escape the notice of his fellow cavalrymen in 1867.

The point of the story is quite clear. Here was a man who spent nearly every day—and up to twenty hours on some days—in the saddle and had already concluded four years of mounted warfare without more than a scratch, yet he lost control long enough to kill his horse with his own weapon. Even though you may ride frequently by today's standards, I would hazard a guess that Custer had years of experience past that which you will achieve on the last day you ever ride. Don't take a chance!

Turning our attention to saddles once more, if you intend to make your saddle do double duty and accommodate a set of panniers as well as your butt, you had better consider the height of the cantle and horn prior to buying a McClellan-style rig with little or none of either. It is also wise to plan for such activities as dragging an animal out of a hard-to-reach area, using the horse to do the pulling. In that situation, a breast collar will be much appreciated. I can recall a time or two when someone hooked onto a good-sized load with a lariat and put the iron to the horse only to have the load stay put while the saddle, rider and all, ended up under the horse. The same result often occurs on steep grades with a fully loaded pack saddle if there is not a breast collar and a breeching (rump strap), or crupper, to keep the load from imparting its own inertia to the saddle. This same basic benefit is gained with a double-rigged saddle as the rear cinch helps keep loads in place and the saddle right side up.

Perhaps this is the proper time to insert another note of interest learned in the school of hard knocks. If you have never tried to lead a pack horse, not to mention a string of them, take heed. No matter how many times you've seen some Tinseltown trapper leading five or six pack animals with an inch-thick rope tied securely to his own saddle, don't do it! Tying a string of horses or mules together with such a stout rope is asking for the loss of every head and all of your outfit if one of the group slips or spooks over the precipice on a mountain pass or into a ravine. Guess what happens if your mount is tied to the pack string when that happens? In the event that you feel it is necessary to tie the pack animals to each other, and to your horse, use something that will snap with a reasonable amount of effort, such as a couple wraps of twine. Any pack animal will follow along as well with a single wrap of the lead rope around your saddle horn, or held in your hand, as it will with the rope snubbed down with a set of square knots.

On the same general topic, it is wise not to allow a packed animal to stop for any length of time while you are on the trail, for the first thing you know, you'll have one major mess as they start lying down and rolling on their packs. It is also not unreasonable to consider basketing your pack animals' muzzles to prevent them from constantly trying to stop and graze while you are attempting to make time on the trail. It only takes one sudden stop caused by such a desire to convince you of the validity of the practice which was once commonplace, but is rapidly on the decline with the newcomers to the packing game.

Saddle blankets versus pads will again stir up a hornet's nest of controversy based on individual preference and practice. While blankets functioned for hundreds of years, there is little doubt that the purpose for which they are intended is better served by a pad. A pad gives more protection to a horse's back while providing a lot more cushion and spring to the rider seated above him. If, however, you have never used a saddle pad before, that same thickness and spring will give you fits for a brief time until you learn the extra amount of tension that needs to be imparted to the cinching procedure to keep the saddle from sliding as you mount and ride. As has been said so often in this book, practice using the equipment before you head off into the woods.

Choosing your ropes can be as confusing as choosing any other equipment, both in terms of material and strength. For anyone who has worked with heavy, braided hemp, and spent time digging slivers of fiber out of his hands afterward, there will be few questions as to why I would not recommend this material for general use. As far as lariats go, the general-duty roping lariat is fine for the purpose it was intended to perform, catching cows. As far as using it to tie loads down, it is both unsuitable and damned expensive. The stiff nature of a lariat does not lend itself well to tight knots without a fight, and once you get one made, the coat-

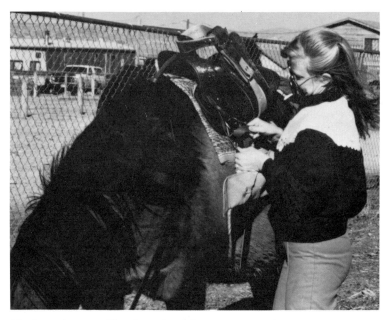

Blankets do not offer the animal the protection of a pad, but are easier to cinch over.

Pads may result in a slipped saddle.

ing on the rope makes it just about impossible ever to untie.

Nylon ropes come in about as many different configurations and sizes as you can imagine, yet some of them are also not much good for packing or tying up with. The cheap nylon ropes in the quarter-inch-diameter category tend to snap too easily to be of much use for anything, and the shiny surface of these same ropes makes it difficult to get them to hold a knot under pressure. You can pick these poor choices out by sight, as they look as if they have been braided from the same plastic that bread sacks are made from. On the other hand, the good nylon ropes appear to have almost the same sheen and consistency of cotton. A rope of one-half inch or so will bear a fantastic load and will tie and untie without much hassle. These are the ones that pay for themselves over the years. Good cotton rope in the inch range is by far the easiest and most satisfying material for use in lead ropes.

If you are going to hang a coiled lariat on your saddle, don't depend on the strap of the saddle to secure it alone. I will bet that at least half of you who try it will find the end of the lariat dragging on the ground in only a few hours of riding, if it takes that long. Since you may not even need the thing, a single wrap with a plastic-coated garbage-bag tie will keep the rope coiled until you do need it, and it only takes a few seconds to get it into use. If you choose not to take this simple precaution, expect the worst: the dragging rope will loop around a snag and when the forward motion of your horse takes the slack out of the coil, you will rip the leather retaining strap from your saddle, at the very least. You could roll the horse and you, in the most extreme case, if the rope also loops the saddle horn.

I said before that you should check to see if the boots you intend to wear hunting fit the stirrups on the saddle and, if not, that you should get a set of oversized stirrups. Now, I'll add another dimension to that task. In the event that you opt for oversized stirrups and the ones you buy are made of cast fiberglass instead of the traditional wood and metal bands, go over them very carefully with your bare hand and check for sharp points, slivers of glass, and casting marks that have not been removed. Any of these that you find should be filed or ground off on a wheel or disc sander to make them smooth. I saw a fine gelding bleeding like someone had taken a razor blade to his flank from such an untended stirrup. Check out what you buy ahead of time.

The admonition to buy sturdy saddlebags in an earlier chapter still holds. No matter how lightweight and handy thin canvas or nylon may seem, I promise you that the motion of the contents as the horse walks will wear a hole in them in one hunt. I have yet to see a set of saddlebags for sale that are too big to be of use. On the opposite end of the scale, however, there are many models which must be intended to carry one sandwich in each pocket. Avoid spending good money for such miniscule showpieces, for they will be of very little value for the purpose of a hunt. Remembering that I said the flaps of the bags should be completely secure on all meeting points with the pockets, I now add a few suggestions to that statement. As handy as Velcro can be, the bonding of flap to pocket of a saddlebag is not one of its better functions, unless used in conjunction with some other type of fasteners. As soon as a stick or other solid object hooks under the edge of the Velcro-hooked flap, the bag opens and the contents begin to spill out. Metal buckles work, but they have been supplanted in my mind by the newer nylon fasteners that pinch together to open and can be adjusted for fit by sliding them up or down on the straps. Not only do they have the advantage of speed in opening and closing, but they are completely silent, thus eliminating the need to tape them over.

While those saddlebags are one of the handiest items that you will take with you on a hunt, they can become a menace by the very nature of the convenient storage they provide. There are certain things which should not go into the saddlebags, and foremost on the list are your survival items like first-aid kit, waterproof matches, a compass, and at least some of your extra ammunition. No one plans to get lost, break a leg, or have an equally disastrous moment, but

Various cartridge carriers lend themselves well to any hunt. You can
carry them on your gun, . . .

. . . on your belt, . . .

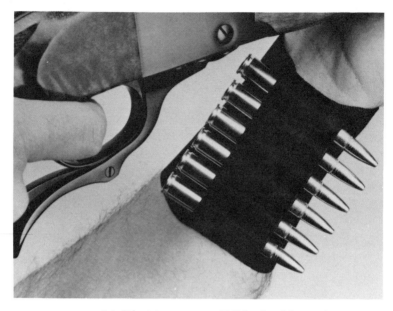

. . . or on your wrist. (Photos courtesy of Michaels of Oregon)

counting on having your horse within reach when such a calamity does befall you is tantamount to expecting the police to be following you around, by chance, when you are mugged. Plan for the unexpected by always carrying on your person those items which can make the difference between life and death. For the horseman, spare ammo is easily carried in numerous belt-loop type carriers, or any other of the multiple possibilities available. The plastic carriers packed inside of Federal cartridge boxes are hard to beat for this purpose. They are light, secure, won't corrode brass like leather, carry ten shells, and cost nothing. What more could you ask?

By the way, the old story about the hunters who got lost and shot into the air three times until they both ran out of arrows, all to no avail, is just about as appropriate when speaking of a firearm user doing the same thing. Think of how many times you have been hunting and heard three spaced shots during the day. Now consider how many of those times you rushed off madly to save the lost hunter doing the shooting. Forget that tactic until well after dark when someone knows that you are in trouble and is looking for you. Even then, one shot and a lot of hollering will do the same job. This is one area where a cheap whistle may be of value to keep you from shouting till you are hoarse. (No pun intended!)

When we considered the strap of the canteen as a definite problem area because of the tendency of the weight to strain the material to the breaking point as the horse moves at faster than a walk, we could have easily substituted binocular cases for canteens. Unless you have a good leather case with a sturdy leather strap which extends completely around the bottom of the case, forget using it on a saddle. Leatherette, plastic, and other substitutes, with the exception of nylon, will be broken and your field glasses will be deposited somewhere on a mountainside. That carrying-case strap should also be adjusted, be it on the binocular case or the canteen, so that the item hangs as close to the point of attachment on the saddle as you can get it. This prevents the canteen or case from bouncing and slapping as the horse moves. Not only does this make the horse less jumpy, but it also keeps noise to a minimum and takes some added strain off the straps by limiting the distance the object moves.

Turning our attention to the bridle and reins, you may once again use whatever suits your fancy, but, as always, there are a few things to consider. One-ear headstalls, without a throat strap, are fine for most purposes, but the hunting horse that may be left unattended for a few hours will learn to slip that headgear off on the nearest tree. Since you already know enough not to expect the reins and bridle to hold a tied horse and have included a halter and lead rope in your plans, this may not seem important. But, given the nature of horses, the next thing that will occur after the bridle slips from the head is for the entire mass of straps and strings to get tangled around the animal's hooves and legs. If a fight develops over that binding, you may end up with a lame nag or even one with a broken leg. Therefore, it is best to remove the bridle when you leave the horse, or get one with a more secure headstall, such as the two-eared, brow-band type that served for years before the one-eared variety gained its present popularity.

When it comes to trailers used for transporting horses, they too may be a breed in themselves. Not that most commercial trailers aren't up to the task, but several things are different about trailering on a logging road as compared to the same job done on the highway. Some of the things to consider prior to trailering on unpaved roads are: is the suspension up to the added burden of dropping 3,000 pounds into a foot-deep hole, and is there enough ground clearance under the rig to pass over projecting rocks or clear one end of a ditch that is nearly straight up and down on each side?

The two most likely areas to hang up a trailer are under the axles, naturally, and at the very rear where the doors are located. The reason is that many trailers are often made to provide for the least amount of "step-up" for the loading animals, and adding to that, the I-beam reinforcement under the door area to bear the weight of the horses stepping in often leaves only three or four inches of ground clearance in that area. Of course, checking the clearance of the trailer while it is empty will be of as much use as checking your body weight on the moon. Put the horses in the trailer and then measure for clearance. That extra 2,000 pounds or so of horseflesh is going to settle the springs considerably.

Still one more commonsense article which, for some strange reason, goes right over a lot of heads, is that any trailer running on rubber tires is subject to flats like anything else. If you don't have at least one spare tire mounted on an appropriate-sized rim to fit the trailer wheels, get one!

The last item I'll mention in regard to trailers is perhaps the most important in that it can cost you a horse. No matter how many miles you have pulled your particular outfit with the animals never suffering a scratch, before you even think about hauling them into the backcountry, go through the interior and eliminate any and all projecting bolts, sharp corners, or other sources of possible lacerations. The tossing around that goes on in a horse trailer in the outback is best illustrated by your effort to remain standing in the box of a pickup truck while it bounces and sways over an unpaved road or field. When that action becomes exaggerated in the trailer, the animals get tossed and thrown with violent force against the walls and doors, and any cutting edge does real damage to the bodies so impaled on them. For the same reason, if you do not have a non-slip floor in the trailer, put one in it.

The next suggestion will probably not be necessary for the majority of hunting horse owners, but since a few tend to forget, I'll throw it in. For the sake of your mount's safety in the forest during big-game season, it is wise to bedeck your tack and the animal's body with some hunter orange. The easiest way to accomplish this is to take a roll of marking tape and apply it to your saddle, scabbard, and saddlebags, along with the halter, mane, and tail of your horse. This tape is sold under various names, but it is nothing more than a ribbon of unglued material, about an inch wide, that can be cut to any length. Strips about sixteen inches long are plenty to separate your companion from the denizens of the wild. It is a sad commentary on the quality of a few hunters to say that taping is a needed addition, but, life being what it is, this is a smart and necessary move.

Well, my friends, you now have the basic information to allow you to plan, prepare for, and complete a hunt on horseback. Be aware that there are still a few hundred things that can go wrong, or fail to work for you. You must consider, plan, test, and, finally, try everything in realistic practice sessions to be sure the techniques and equipment work for you in any given situation. I hope that I have helped you over the first few hurdles and you can now fly by yourself.

Appendix A

Fish & Game Departments

T he following list provides fish and game department information in the U.S. and Canada, current at the time of publication based on data provided by each state and province that responded to a questionnaire. To make the best use of the listings, first decide where you would like to hunt, and for what species. When that is clear, contact the appropriate agencies for license, regulation, and season information. Based on normal permit quotas and drawing times, it is wise to query state agencies at least a year in advance.

The following fish and game department addresses are provided with three "question columns" for use as a quick reference when planning your hunt.

KEY

Column number:

1. Does the state or province require guides and outfitters to be licensed before they may conduct business? Yes or No.

2. Does the state require any tests be passed before a license is issued to guides or outfitters? Yes or No.

3. Does the state make available lists of licensed guides and outfitters on request from sportsmen? Yes or No.

NA indicates no answer received.

In some states, no license is required, or a license is optional, or the operator has provided a name to the department for release to potential clients without being licensed. Most lists are free; however, some states may charge for them. They should inform you of any cost that exists prior to sending the listing.

UNITED STATES

	1	2	3
Alabama Department of Conservation Division of Game and Fish 62 N. Union St. Montgomery, AL 36130	Yes	No	No
Alaska Department of Fish and Game Subport Bldg. Juneau, AK 99801	Yes	Yes	Yes
Arizona Department of Fish and Game 2222 W. Greenway Phoenix, AZ 85023	Yes	Yes	Yes
Arkansas Game and Fish Commission #2 Natural Resources Dr. Little Rock, AR 72205	Yes	No	No
California Department of Fish and Game 1416 9th St. Sacramento, CA 95814	Yes	No	Yes

	1	2	3
Colorado Game, Fish, and Parks Division 6060 Broadway Denver, CO 80216	Yes	Yes	Yes
Connecticut Wildlife Bureau 165 Capitol Ave. Hartford, CT 06106	No	No	No
Delaware Division of Fish and Wildlife P.O. Box 1401 Dover, DE 19903	No	No	Yes
Florida Division of Game and Fresh Water Fish 620 S. Meridian Tallahassee, FL 32304	No	No	No
Georgia Game and Fish Division Floyd Towers East, Suite 1362 205 Butler St. S.E. Atlanta, GA 30334	No	No	No
Hawaii Division of Forestry & Wildlife 1151 Punchbowl St. Honolulu, HI 96813	No	No	Yes
Idaho Outfitters and Guides Board 1365 North Orchard, Room 372 Boise, ID 83706	Yes	Yes	Yes

	1	2	3
Illinois Department of Wildlife Resources 600 N. Grand Avenue West Suite 6 Springfield, IL 62706	No	No	No
Indiana Department of Natural Resources Division of Fish and Game 607 State Office Bldg. Indianapolis, IN 46204	No	No	No
Iowa State Conservation Commission Henry A. Wallace Bldg. Des Moines, IA 50319	No	No	No
Kansas Forestry, Fish, and Game Commission Box 54A, RR 2 Pratt, KS 67124	No	No	No
Kentucky Department of Fish and Wildlife Resources #1 Game Farm Rd. Frankfort, KY 40601	Yes	Yes	No
Louisiana Wildlife and Fisheries Commission P.O. Box 15570 Baton Rouge, LA 70895	No	No	Yes
Maine Inland Fisheries and Wildlife Department 284 State St. Augusta, ME 04333	Yes	Yes	No

	1	2	3
Maryland Department of Natural Resources Tawes State Office Bldg. Annapolis, MD 21401	Yes	No	Yes
Massachusetts Division of Fisheries and Wildlife 100 Cambridge St. Boston, MA 02202	No	No	No
Michigan Department of Natural Resources Mason Bldg. Box 30028 Lansing, MI 48926	No	No	No
Minnesota Department of Natural Resources License Bureau 500 Lafayette Rd., Box 26 St. Paul, MN 55146	Yes	No	Yes
Mississippi Department of Wildlife Conservation P.O. Box 451 Jackson, MS 39205	No	No	No
Missouri Department of Conservation P.O. Box 180 2901 W. Truman Blvd. Jefferson City, MO 65102	No	No	No
Montana Department of Fish, Wildlife, and Parks 1420 E. Sixth Ave. Helena, MT 59620	Yes	Yes	Yes

	1	2	3
Nebraska Game and Parks Commission 2200 N. 33rd Lincoln, NE 68503	No	No	No
Nevada Department of Wildlife P.O. Box 10678 1100 Valley Rd. Reno, NV 89520	Yes	No	Yes
New Hampshire Fish and Game Department 34 Bridge St. Concord, NH 03301	Yes	Yes	Yes
New Jersey Division of Fish, Game, and Wildlife Box 409, RD Hampton, NJ 08827	No	No	Yes
New Mexico Department of Game and Fish Villagra Bldg. Santa Fe, NM 87503	No	No	Yes
New York State Department of Environmental Conservation 50 Wolf Rd. Room 408 Albany, NY 12233	Yes	Yes	Yes
North Carolina Wildlife Resource Commission 512 N. Salsbury St. Raleigh, NC 27611	No	No	No

	1	2	3
North Dakota State Game and Fish Department 100 N. Bismarck Expressway Bismarck, ND 58501	Yes	No	Yes
Ohio Department of Natural Resources Division of Wildlife Fountain Square Bldg. C Columbus, OH 43224	No	No	No
Oklahoma Department of Wildlife Conservation 1801 No. Lincoln P.O. Box 53465 Oklahoma City, OK 73152	No	No	No
Oregon State Marine Board 3000 Market St. N.E. #505 Salem, OR 97310	Yes	Yes	Yes
Pennsylvania Fish Commission P.O. Box 1673 Harrisburg, PA 17105	No	No	No
Rhode Island Division of Fish and Wildlife Government Center, Tower Hill Rd. Wakefield, RI 02879	No	No	No
South Carolina Wildlife Resources Department P.O. Box 167 Columbia, SC 29202	No	No	No

	1	2	3
South Dakota Department of Game, Fish, and Parks 445 E. Capital Pierre, SD 57501	No	No	Yes
Tennessee Wildlife Resources Agency P.O. Box 40747 Nashville, TN 37204	No	No	No
Texas Parks and Wildlife Department 4200 Smith School Rd. Austin, TX 78744	Yes	No	Yes
Utah Division of Wildlife Resources 1596 W.N. Temple Salt Lake City, UT 84116	No	No	Yes
Vermont Fish and Wildlife Department 103 S. Main St. Montpelier, VT 05676	No	No	No
Virginia Commission of Game and Inland Fisheries 4010 W. Broad St. Box 11104 Richmond, VA 23230	No	No	No
Washington Department of Game 600 N. Capitol Way Olympia, WA 98504	No	No	Yes

	1	2	3
West Virginia Department of Natural Resources 1800 Washington St. E. Charleston, WV 25305	Yes	No	Yes
Wisconsin Department of Natural Resources Box 7924 Madison, WI 53707	Yes	No	Yes
Wyoming Game and Fish Department Box 1589 Cheyenne, WY 82002	Yes	Yes	Yes

CANADA

	1	2	3
Alberta Fish and Wildlife Division Petroleum Plaza 9945-108 Street Edmonton T5K 2C9	Yes	Yes	Yes
British Columbia Ministry of Environment Wildlife Branch 780 Blanshard St. Victoria V8V 1X5	Yes	No	Yes
Manitoba Department of Natural Resources P.O. Box 22 1495 St. James St. Winnipeg R3H 0W9	Yes	Yes	Yes

	1	2	3
New Brunswick Department of Natural Resources P.O. Box 6000 Fredericton E3B 5H1	Yes	Yes	Yes
Newfoundland Wildlife Division Bldg. 810 Pleasantville St. John's A1A 1P9	Yes	Yes	Yes
Northwest Territories Government of the Northwest Territories Box 1320 Yellowknife X1A 2L9	Yes	Yes	Yes
Nova Scotia Department of Lands and Forests P.O. Box 698 Halifax B3J 2T9	Yes	Yes	Yes
Ontario Ministry of Natural Resources Room 1640 99 Wellesly St. West Toronto M7A 1W3	Yes	No	Yes
Prince Edward Island Department of Community & Cultural Affairs P.O. Box 2000 Charlottetown C1A 7N8	No	No	Yes
Quebec Department of Loisir Chasse et Peche 150 St. Cyrile St. Quebec City Quebec G1R 4Y1	Yes	No	Yes

	1	2	3
Saskatchewan Resource Lands Branch Box 3003 Prince Albert S6V 6G1	Yes	No	Yes
Yukon Territory Department of Renewable Resources Box 2703 Whitehorse Y1A 4A4	Yes	Yes	Yes

Appendix B
Guides & Outfitters Associations

The following list offers the names and addresses of associations in the United States and Canada which provide listings of guides and outfitters in their particular areas. Once you have contacted the fish and game departments for information on licenses, seasons, and regulations, then contact these agencies for information on guides and outfitters who specialize in the type of hunt you wish to make.

This information is current at the time of publication and based on data provided by each state and province that responded to a questionnaire. Based on normal permit quotas and drawing times, it is wise to query state agencies at least a year in advance.

UNITED STATES

Alabama
None

Alaska
Professional Hunters Association
P.O. Box 441
Talkeetna, AK 99676

Arizona
None

Arkansas
None

California
None

Colorado
Colorado Outfitters Association
1759 S. Ironton
Aurora, CO 80012

Connecticut
None

Delaware
None

Florida
None

Georgia
None

Hawaii
None

Idaho
Outfitters and Guides Association
P.O. Box 95
Boise, ID 83701

Illinois
None

Indiana
None

Iowa
None

Kansas
None

Kentucky
None

Louisiana
None

Maine
Maine Professional Guides Association
Box 265
Medway, ME 04460

Maryland
None

Massachusetts
None

Michigan
None

Minnesota
None

Mississippi
None

Missouri
None

Montana
Montana Outfitters and Guides Association
P.O. Box 631
Hot Springs, MT 59845

Nebraska
None

Nevada
Wilde Brough
Nevada Outfitters and Guides
Clover Valley
Wells, NV 89835

New Hampshire
None

New Jersey
None

New Mexico
New Mexico Council of Outfitters and Guides, Inc.
P.O. Box 994
Socorro, NM 87801

New York
N.Y.S. Outdoor Guides Association
P.O. Box 4337
Albany, NY 12204

North Carolina
NA

North Dakota
None

Ohio
None

Oklahoma
None

Oregon
None

Pennsylvania
None

Rhode Island
None

South Carolina
None

South Dakota
None

Tennessee
None

Texas
None

Utah
None

Vermont
None

Virginia
None

Washington
Washington Guides and Outfitters Association
P.O. Box 108
Issaquah, WA 98207

West Virginia
Eastern Professional Outfitters
P.O. Box 127
Barboursville, WV 25504

Wisconsin
None

Wyoming
Wyoming Outfitters Association
P.O. Box 4194
Jackson Hole, WY 83001

CANADA AND TERRITORIAL AGENCIES

Alberta
Outfitters Association
Box 511
Claresholm T0L 0T0

British Columbia
Guide and Outfitter Association
Box 759
100 Mile House V0K 2E0

Manitoba
Outfitters Association
Box 304
Churchhill R0B 0E0

New Brunswick
Outfitters Association
RR 2
Doaktown E0G 1G0

Newfoundland
Outfitters Association
P.O. Box 9
Corner Break A2H 6C3

Northwest Territories
None

Nova Scotia
Hunting & Fishing Guides Association
4 Virginia Ave.
Truro
Colchester Co. B2N 2N6

Ontario
Northern Ontario Tourist Outfitters Association
P.O. Box 1140
North Bay P1B 8K4

Prince Edward Island
None

Quebec
L'Association des Pourvoyeurs
2900 boul. St. Martin Ouest
Chomedey, Laval H7T 2J2

Saskatchewan
Outfitters Association
P.O. Box 2016
Prince Albert S6V 6K1

Yukon
Outfitters Association
P.O. Box 4840
Whitehorse Y1A 4N6